Persepolis, from Glasgow

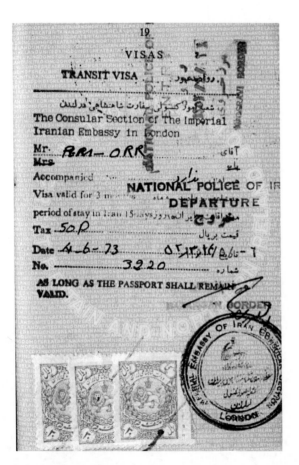

Visa for Iran

Visa for Iraq

Persepolis from Glasgow
in a school bus
with stops on the way

Richard M. Orr

Kennedy & Boyd

Kennedy & Boyd
an imprint of
Zeticula Ltd
Unit 13,
196 Rose Street,
Edinburgh,
EH2 4AT

http://www.kennedyandboyd.co.uk
admin@kennedyandboyd.co.uk

First published 2016:
Text and Photographs Copyright © Richard M. Orr 2016
Cover photograph: The School Bus at Ctesiphon: South wing and vault of Sasanid palace

ISBN 978-1-84921-162-8

Preface

Step back with me, if you will, to 1973 when Marshal Tito controlled Jugoslavia, the Shah was enthroned in Iran and Saddam Hussein was vice president in Iraq. Come along with our group of students and teachers on a Glasgow school bus safari through Turkey to Persepolis in the heart of Persia.

The trip covered 11,500 miles over a period of 6 weeks and included visits to many important archaeological sites such as Troy, Ephesus, Nimrud Dagi and Babylon before reaching our goal at Persepolis.

Political relations in the various countries were certainly volatile but we never felt threatened. Armed forces too figured prominently in some areas but were usually supportive and interested in our expedition. Considering the map today, it is clear that such a trip could not happen.

The scale of damage done recently to many of the places we visited that summer of 1973 is appalling. After a series of well publicised acts of barbarism on its supposed enemies, the militant organisation —known, as I write, as Islamic State —has turned its attention in recent months to wiping out traces of earlier cultures and their beliefs. Armed with picks and bulldozers, so-called IS moved first against mosques and shrines and went on to attack the walls at Nineveh, Ashurnasirpal's palace at Nimrud, and areas in Hatra. Mosul's museum has been attacked and plundered and now Palmyra (which we visited with another trip in 1972) is being targeted and despoiled. Antiquities looted during these unconscionable attacks are sold to dealers to finance their activities.

To be sure, our own record in Britain during the Reformation in the 16th century —with its wanton destruction of art and books in churches and monasteries — is bad, but the threat by so-called Islamic State is far more extensive. We must hope that this pernicious and destructive force is soon eliminated, allowing visits to these fascinating sites to resume.

Richard Orr
Spring 2016

Contents

Illustrations

Ready to roll: the gang gathers in Glasgow city centre

The Background

More than forty years ago, when Marshal Tito still controlled Jugoslavia as president, when Saddam Hussein was Vice president in Iraq and had just escaped an attempted assassination, and when the Shah still held power in Iran, I set off from Glasgow with a group of teachers, students and senior pupils on a journey which could not be replicated today and travelled through a very different political landscape. I invite you to join me as I recount that trip from the pages of my diary, supported by selected photographs of the many places we visited.

Travel has always been a delight for me and, right from the time of my entry into teaching, and having adjusted to the ending of my eight memorable years as purser on the Clyde turbine steamers *Marchioness of Graham* and *Queen Mary II*, educational travel has been part of my *modus operandi*. Starting out from humble beginnings like annual Easter walking holidays with school groups on Hadrian's Wall using youth hostels for accommodation, I progressed quickly to a more adventurous school visit in 1968 with pupils from the High School of Glasgow to Greek and Roman sites in Italy, using rail passes and youth hostels to effect our itinerary. Before embarking on this venture, I tested the ground with Ian, a trusted friend of long standing, and used trains and hostels to tour both Italy and Sicily. Certainly, there was a lot of walking from rail station to hostel and the occasional missing of trains hidden away at unlikely places in stations, but we reckoned it was proved to be practicable and so we took the plunge. Then came a tour of Tunisia in an old, somewhat erratic Bedford dormobile with four of us, all graduates, sharing costs - unfortunately, we timed the trip so as nearly to coincide with the Israeli Six Day war in 1967. Still, ignoring official advice, we went ahead and weathered this time of hostility with merely a minor stoning outside the Roman site at Maktar - an elderly Arab drove away the youngsters responsible - and I was sufficiently emboldened (or deranged) to undertake that school trip to Italy the following year.

My next undertaking in 1969 was more ambitious - a lengthy linear passage from Algeria, over Tunisia and right across Libya, visiting such major Roman sites as Timgad, Djemila and Lambaesis in Algeria, as well as tiny Tiddis at the back of beyond as being family home of Lollius Urbicus, Governor of Britain under the Roman emperor Antoninus Pius and responsible for creating our Antonine Wall back home in Scotland. We then travelled on to wonder at the incredible Sabratha, Lepcis Magna and Cyrene in Libya, before just succeeding to evade Gaddafi's coup and seizure of power from King Idris and sailing for Sicily. On this particular trip, we numbered but two, my pal Ian and myself, and hired a new Vauxhall Viva to serve as our travelling hotel, complete with foam mattress and home made curtains for a sort of privacy. We named her Livia Viva and she performed famously, even faultlessly. This was fortuitous. Before setting out, we had requested and obtained from the hirer an enlarged emergency repair kit but this was stolen on the ferry crossing to Algiers. We had been instructed to leave our vehicle unlocked and never imagined that the tool kit would be a target! Not that it could have helped us much with the sand which all but swamped the engine as we tracked down Roman olive farms well off the beaten track. Greece was my destination for 1970 at the head of a group of High School former pupils. We relied on public transport to visit island and mainland sites and slept on rooftops, beaches and lawns where hostels failed us. Naturally, we made a splendid target for mosquitoes when sleeping in the open! Next year's trip was a calmer affair, thanks to hiring a minibus from Ostend to take our party to sites in Greece and Turkey.

But 1972 proved a real test: an educational foray taking 6 students and 4 adults across Turkey into Syria and Jordan to see such striking classical sites as Palmyra, Jerash and Petra. This would have been tricky in the best of conditions but the vehicle, a large clapped out Land Rover hired to take us from Istanbul, proved disastrous. We were two days late departing, owing to problems with the vehicle's dodgy differential. This was a mere introduction and there followed loss of a wheel while speeding along the highway and narrowly avoiding going over a ravine as we slewed across the road with our rucsacs bouncing along the highway behind us, then various minor mishaps culminating in a memorable meander through the Syrian desert, coating us all with yellow dust which poured in through the many gaps in our bodywork and transformed us into desert rat look alikes, and finally total breakdown for 5 days in Damascus with clutch failure. Faced with this crisis, the party split, half of us travelling to Jordan by bus and taxi to see Jerash and spectacular Petra and proceeding thence by bus to visit Beirut and Baalbek in Lebanon. After all, this *had* been the original plan, assuming we had a roadworthy vehicle. There, in Lebanon, we rejoined our wretched Land Rover and saw Tyre and Sidon before travelling back through Turkey via several other important classical sites. We gladly took our leave of the vehicle at Alexandroupolis. By this time the smell of oil inside was appalling and the rear door had developed an alarming tendency to fly open quite unexpectedly. You might suppose that the 1972 experience would have turned me against such far-flung expeditions. But the reverse was the case. I refused to believe that anything so alarming and demanding could recur - lightning does not strike twice - and proceeded boldly with the next scheme.

Thus were the foundations laid for a momentous overland excursion in 1973 to see Persepolis at the heart of the ancient Persian empire. The underlying purpose of the trip was to provide background material for a new course in Classical studies which, in my capacity as Adviser in Classics, I was preparing for Glasgow schools, but the scheme soon took on a momentum of its own.

RECOMMENDED GEAR

FOREIGN TRAVEL — EXTENDED STAY

CLOTHES FOR TRAVEL: Jacket/anorak etc for pocket space
PAPERS/DOCUMENTS: Youth Hostel Card   Passport and any Medical Certificate
                     Student Identity Card Travellers' cheques (as desired)
                     Currency (foreign?)   Emergency reserve (£10?)
                           Money Belt/Wallet(s)

KIT WILL BEST BE CARRIED IN RUCKSACK

SMALL CARRIER (duffel bag/satchel) is helpful.

Richard Orr.
(1971 Passport Photograph)

MINIMUM

1 Long trouser
1 Shorts
1 Swim-trunks
1 Vest
3 Sports Shirts
1 "dress" shirt and tie
1 Walking shoes
1 Sandshoes/sandals/old plimsolls
1 Sunhat
1 Sweater/jersey
1 Pyjamas
1 Sheet Sleeping Bag and lilo/
  "unmanageable"/air pillow?
3 pair light socks
3 pair underpants

  spare plimsolls

MINIMUM

1 Plastic/nylon coat
  Handkerchiefs
2 Towels
1 Dish-cloth
  Toilet Paper
  Soap powder/CAKE soap
1 Wash kit (nail & tooth **brush**/metal
  mirror) + extra soap and toothpaste
  String and clothes pegs
  Plate, mug and cutlery
  Sunspectacles (preferably Polaroid)
  Sun tan lotions
MEDICAL KIT eg Magnesia tablets/entero-
vioform/laxative/antihistamine cream —
insect repellent/Iodine OR TCP OR Dettol
OR antiseptic/plaster/bandages/water
purifying tablets?/salt tablets?/throat
and eye salve.

ALSO HIGHLY RECOMMENDED

Torch
Sink plug
Plastic water bottle
Tin opener
Hussif (needle and thread)
Guide Book/Phrase Book etc

WHERE APPLICABLE

Shaving gear
Shoe-cleaning kit
Camera and plenty film
Spare Spectacles
Writing Gear/Diary

Left.
This served as a standard
guide for my trips abroad
hence the reference to train
food

FOOD FOR TRAIN

Include eg fruit/juices/cheese/nuts/raisins/biscuits/rice/tinned fish/meat.

Adv/Classics/RMO/MH
19 Apr 73

4

The Project

Our goal was Persepolis, ceremonial capital of the great king Darius of Persia and his son and successor Xerxes. To achieve this, we planned to follow Persia's Royal Road from its starting point at Sardis in modern Turkey, proceed by Konya through the Cilician Gates in the Taurus Mountains, head westwards by Mosul in Iraq, then take the direction of the River Tigris south to ancient Babylon and thereafter visit Persia's administrative capital at Susa, before heading for our terminus at Persepolis. This was the famous road known to Persian messengers, travelled by Xenophon and the Ten Thousand Greeks and later used by Alexander the Great in his destructive march to Persepolis. It looked plain sailing on the maps and ideal support for our envisaged school topic "The Greeks and the Persians". After all, it was Darius who instigated the ill-starred invasion of Athens to punish the Greeks for interference in his domain. This was rebuffed at Marathon in 490 BC and Darius died soon after. Then it fell to his son Xerxes to lead an even greater punitive expedition against the Greeks and to suffer even greater humiliation when his fleet was defeated at Salamis in 480 BC and then his army met a similar fate at Plataea. Persepolis, owing its origin to Darius and Xerxes, seemed the obvious goal for our expedition.

Naturally enough, we passed numerous places, either on the road or in cities we visited, which would have been well worth devoting some time to seeing. Turkey, Iraq and Iran were festooned with significant archaeological sites and so we had to cut our cloth carefully. We kept fairly close to our planned itinerary, deviating only where road conditions required a rethink. We also tried to include a few really outstanding places, such as Nemrut Dağı, Hatra (events brought this about) and Istanbul, when they were within reasonably easy reach of our chosen route and considered worthy of our attention. I was responsible for planning the sites which we would visit and used the Hachette Guides to Turkey and to The Middle East as my sources. They were excellent for my purpose and provided a mine of information in advance of as well as during the trip. Even today, they are a joy to study thanks to the detailed coverage.

Belgian Customs

THE CORPORATION OF GLASGOW—EDUCATION DEPARTMENT

MEMORANDUM

From: Mr Kydd SAA Department	*To:* Mr Orr Adviser in Classics

Ref: RK/IG   15 May 1973

The Education Committee on Friday 11 May agreed to give a guarantee of £4,563 to the Iran Government in the event of the High School minibus being lost through wilful neglect or by intent during its passage through Iran. The Corporation will in turn require a statement from you and the other members of your party that you will refund them the money if in fact the vehicle is lost through wilful neglect or by intent. The Town Clerk would therefore like to have a list of the names and addresses of all members of the party. If you will let me have that I shall pass it on to him.

The terms of the guarantee from Glasgow Corporation

Preparations and Problems

Events soon showed that it was not to be plain sailing! Early in 1973, the planning got under way. My Classics colleague at Queens Park Secondary took on plotting the route while I, by virtue of my recent appointment as full time Classics adviser to Glasgow schools, undertook to assemble a party and find the transport. Few schools rushed to offer a minibus, but out of the blue came David Lees, rector of the High School of Glasgow and a strong supporter of Classics. I knew him well, as I had been both pupil and teacher in the school and he had encouraged me in each capacity in my desire to charter the Clyde paddle steamer *Caledonia* to take the school to Brodick on the Isle of Arran, first in 1957 and again in 1967. Both outings were well supported and voted a great success. You will note this early evidence of my fondness for organising trips! It so happened that a second, new bus had been lately acquired for the school and David was willing to offer this to enable the trip to proceed. The bus was a blue Ford, with tasteful lettering proclaiming ownership by The High School of Glasgow.

So the bus problem was resolved but other obstacles soon followed. Restrictions on the importing of Ford vehicles into Arab countries had to be addressed, hostilities between Iraq and Iran and unrest in Kurdistan gave us concern, which the Foreign Office in London could not allay as they seemed little wiser than ourselves, reliable reports on road conditions were hard to find, and stringent visa requirements for our passage through various countries had to be met - Iran and Iraq were the main offenders, the latter handled by the Royal Afghan Embassy London, Iraqi Interests Section, since Britain had no diplomatic relations with Iraq at the time. (We were not to know that there would be an unsuccessful coup in Iraq just as we set out, nor that Afghanistan's Shah would fall to a coup in July resulting in his stepping down in August! We chose a turbulent time.) Then came the need to secure a broker to insure the venture and, the *pièce de resistance*, a guarantor to stand surety for £4,500 in the event of our failure to take the vehicle back out of Iran. In this last crisis, Glasgow Corporation came to our aid, thanks to our Director's pleading at the Education Sub Committee in May. After all, they expected us to return, and so Glasgow Education assumed the mantle of our bankers!

Next came the mustering of the party. This was much harder than usual because of the distance and time. Normally, I had to select from a crowd of wannabes but on this occasion I had a real search on my hands. School pupils were not up for it - perhaps it was just too much of an adventure! So I increased the number of adults to compensate. As route planner and main driver, Donald, my Classics colleague, was a key figure. He had also experienced and survived our Syrian venture as a fellow passenger the previous year on that atrocious hired Land Rover. He was certain he could do better and I was confident that he could not do worse! Then came my reliable and well tried fellow traveller Ian. As I have earlier noted, he was a constant companion on my various educational ploys: Tunisia, Libya, Syria, and Turkey among others. Besides, he was like me a former pupil of the High School. Donald enlisted a science colleague from Queens Park Secondary as co-driver and, more important, to see to repair and maintenance of the vehicle should need arise. This seemed an essential consideration in view of recent experience! Bill the mechanic was joined by another scientist, also named Bill, whom I cajoled into joining the trip from Hillpark Secondary. His remit was taking charge of visas, camping gear and, at the last moment, the medical chest. This last imposition resulted from the withdrawal on departure day of our sole medical student, a recent High School pupil, who thus reduced our party size from our target of twelve to eleven souls. For easier identification of each Bill, our co-driver will usually appear as Billco while Hillpark

Bill will be named Hillbill. Two students recently from the High also joined the group. First Roger, a geologist who found much to interest himself and us in our travels - he had also survived my 1971 excursion to Greece and Turkey, so knew what to expect! Better still, he also kept a diary and we have maintained contact over the years. His is a different perspective and I have incorporated some of his reactions in my account of the trip. Campbell was the other, a law student and chess devotee. Our party was completed by four genuine school pupils, George, a big easy going lad from Greenock, and three Allan Glens Secondary seniors, Douglas, David and Alasdair, the last of whom had a special interest in ancient battles and warfare.

So the scene was set for our departure on 30th June. Necessary injections were organised in May, hurried meetings were held and circulars distributed regarding travel needs and probable cash requirements, and, relief beyond belief, the signed indemnity for the vehicle was received from the Education department on 20th June. Everything seemed to be in place and I was relaxed enough to conduct two coachloads of senior Glasgow pupils around Roman sites as far south as Fishbourne Roman palace in the weeks immediately before our departure.

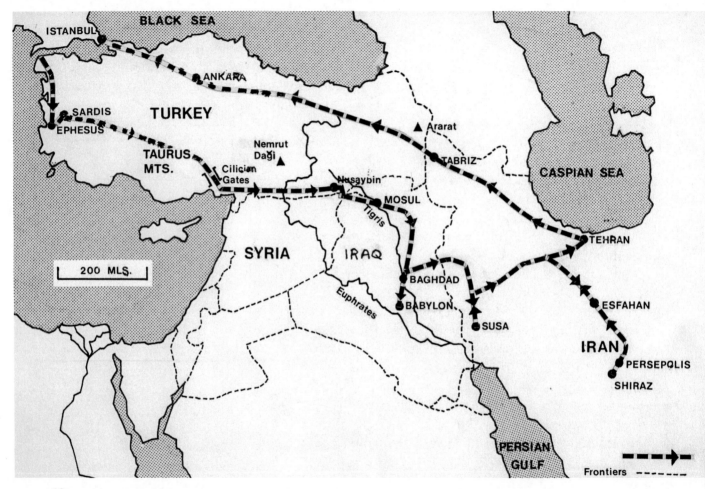

BLACK SEA

ISTANBUL

ANKARA

TURKEY

SARDIS
EPHESUS

TAURUS
MTS.

Cilician
Gates

Nemrut
Daǧi

Ararat

TABRIZ

CASPIAN SEA

Nusaybin

MOSUL

Tigris

SYRIA

IRAQ

TEHRAN

Euphrates

BAGHDAD

BABYLON

SUSA

ESFAHAN

IRAN

PERSEPOLIS

SHIRAZ

PERSIAN
GULF

200 MLS.

Frontiers -------

Pre Travel Information

So to the diary of our travels. But before we embark on the diary, a brief description of how we distributed ourselves around the bus and occupied ourselves during travel will probably prove helpful. On board the bus, Donald and his co-driver colleague Billco took the seat at the front while Douglas, David and Alasdair, the trio from Allan Glens, were invariably to be found positioned at the rear seat. Roger, Campbell and I usually sat in the three seats behind the driver while opposite us were ranged Hillbill, George and Ian. Of us all, George was most likely to move around, but then he liked to sleep when travelling and was intent on finding the place most suited to his somnolence. We employed our sleeping bags to advantage as additional comforters over long distances and they performed this task admirably. George was far the most dedicated sleeper but most of us succumbed from time to time on the trip. Donald (when not driving!), Roger and I were least likely to doze off, but on rare occasions the whole busload apart from the driver were to be found rolling about in the grip of sleep.

So far as ways of passing time were concerned, if we were not sleeping like George or watching the landscape and life in the countries through which we were passing, card play was the chief pastime, solo and contract whist being most common. For some strange reason, Roger had jettisoned the two jokers from the pack at the outset - perhaps, as being the obvious joker in our pack, he feared the competition? In the course of the trip, we lost one other card but were able to find ways round this. Chess was the other chief involvement. Campbell was a keen chess player but met his match in Roger. Alasdair, David and Douglas occasionally played too, but the inexplicable loss of the bishop was an irritation. Reading paperbacks came increasingly into its own on the return trip.

ROYAL SWEDISH EMBASSY
British Interests Section
BAGHDAD

R M Orr Esq
Education Department
Education Offices
129 Bath Street
Glasgow C2

Your reference

Our reference   CON 30/2

Date   21 May 1973

Dear Mr Orr

Thank you for your recent letter about your trip by mini-bus to Iraq
and Iran.

You do not mention if your trip is being arranged privately or commercially
and I shall therefore assume that it is the former. The main roads in
Iraq are well-surfaced and driving conditions are generally good.
Temperatures in July will be high, usually averaging over 110°, and you
should therefore not expect to be able to walk about during the day for
any length of time. There are plenty of fairly cheap and comparatively
clean hotels and government rest houses in or near all the main areas of
archaeological sites in Iraq and accommodation is usually available.
Iraqis welcome tourists and you should not experience any problems or
difficulties during your time here.

You will no doubt have thought of the following points, but they are the
ones that I usually cover when I offer advice to British travellers:

    a. apply for Iraqi entry visas at once;

    b. ensure that you have a carnet de passage for your bus;

    c. purchase at the Iraqi border compulsory third party insurance.
        This is legally required and is additional to any other cover
        which you may arrange; and

    d. do not wear shorts in public - Moslems are sensitive on this
        point.

I hope you will have a pleasant trip and if you have time when in Baghdad
I shall be pleased to see you. Please do not hesitate to write to me again
if you think I can be of further assistance.

                     Yours sincerely

                     W I Rae
                     Consular Attaché

*"(he says nothing of need for Birth Certificate or letter
from a Minister of Religion; nor need for a bankers'
reference; nor queries even Ford buses"*

12

British Embassy
Tehran

Richard M Orr Esq
Corporation of Glasgow
Education Department
Education Offices
129 Bath Street
GLASGOW C2

Your reference   Adv/Classics/RMO/AP

Our reference   31/8

Date   24 May 1973

Dear Mr Orr

I am writing in reply to your letter of 8 May about your
proposed visit to Iran in July.

I think you will find that the enclosed leaflet will answer
most of your general travel queries. If you intend to enter
Iran from Iraq there is only one border crossing point open
at the moment: that at Kosravi (on the Iranian side) which
lies on your route from Thanaquin. Most major roads in Iran
linking the larger towns have good tarmac surfaces; off the
main roads one is usually on hard-packed earth for which a
Land Rover or similar vehicle is preferable. You must be
in possession of a valid "carnet de passages en douanes" for
your mini-bus. At the border the details of the vehicle will
be entered in the passport of a member of the party (usually
the driver's) to ensure the export of the vehicle. Third
party insurance must be obtained locally; the branch of Bank
Melli at Kosravi can issue this on your application there.
All drivers of the bus will have to hold international driving
permits.

Driving in Iran is hazardous to say the least. On main roads
one must treat heavy trucks and buses with respect. They are
driven at high speeds and, in the hands of a poor driver, they
become lethal weapons. Road accidents are frequent. If you
have the misfortune to be involved in a serious accident in
which someone is injured or killed you must be prepared for the
driver to be placed in police detention. Before the detainee
is released compensation must be paid to the injured person or
to the relatives of the deceased. In short - drive carefully.

All members of the party, if travelling on United Kingdom passport
will require entry visas. These can be obtained from the
Iranian Consulate, 50 Kensington Court, London W8. Valid
certificates against smallpox and cholera should be held. A TAB
vaccination is also recommended.

You should have no difficulty in visiting archaeological sites
in Iran. No prior permission is required and access to sites
is easy.

May I wish you and your party a pleasant and interesting visit.

                     Yours sincerely

                     K J Nelson.

Travel Diary

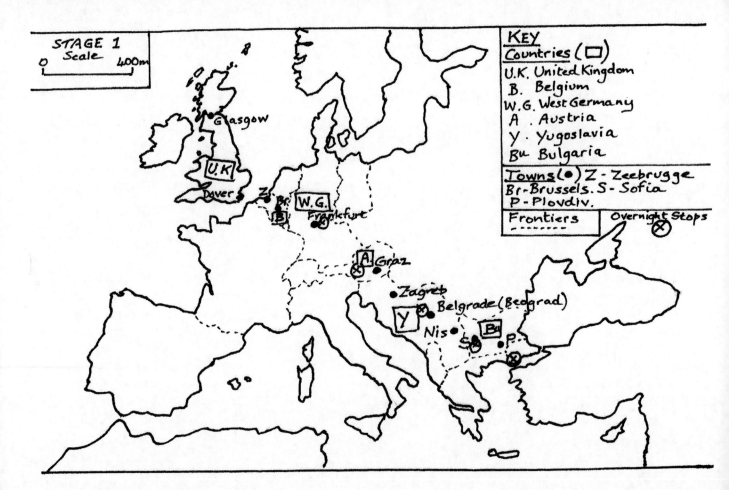

STAGE 1

Scale
0   400m

KEY

Countries (▢)

U.K. United Kingdom
B. Belgium
W.G. West Germany
A . Austria
Y . Yugoslavia
Bu Bulgaria

Towns (●) Z - Zeebrugge
Br - Brussels. S - Sofia
P - Plovdiv.

Frontiers   Overnight Stops
- - - - - - -   ⊗

Glasgow

U.K

Dover
Z
Br
W.G.
B
Frankfurt

A Graz
⊗

Zagreb

Belgrade (Beograd)
⊗

Nis
S
Bu
P.
⊗

14

Stage 1

Saturday 30 June - Wednesday 4 July

Glasgow to Belgium, Germany, Austria, Jugoslavia, Bulgaria

I was up prompt at 7.30 to freshen myself for our first day on the road. We assembled in sunshine at Dundas Vale Teacher Centre in Cowcaddens, where I was met by our intending medical student with the news that he was pulling out. I was naturally less than happy, but at least he had the guts to appear and deliver the bombshell in person! The party dropped to ten, though our eleventh awaited us at Manchester. We got under way at 10.00, after loading our tents and kit on the roof. Hillbill immediately proved his worth in this undertaking and had things on the roof secure and ship shape in next to no time. We stopped briefly past Carlisle at Southwaite Services, which we found grubby and ill managed, but perhaps served as a foretaste of what we might expect in the course of the trip. Manchester treated us to a street pageant and we were quickly caught up in an unexpected procession, as part of Stretford's annual festival, which delayed us for almost two hours. Still, Ian was there waiting patiently to complete our number and we set off again with only a brief stop on the North Circular near the Dartford Tunnel for a late Chinese dinner around 10.00 pm. Dover greeted us at 1am where we boarded Townsend ferry *Free*

Enterprise V for Belgium. We sailed at 2.35 am and Ian and I spent much of the crossing in discussion.

I note that Roger comments favourably on the flower festooned exteriors of pubs in the south of Britain, contrasting with the rather sombre facades to be found in Glasgow's hostelries, as well as on difficulty experienced getting recognition of his Scottish pound notes. This observation has a timeless quality about it!

Sunday brought a new month and the start of our long haul across the continent. We were informed that new travel arrangements were in place but regrettably no one could say what these were. So, after a swift breakfast stop aboard the ship, we passed through Zeebrugge customs at 7 am and proceeded to the autobahn. The roads were already crowded with insane local drivers dashing and crashing in their mad rush to get to the coast. We managed to be through Brussels by 8.30, at which time it was said that both lanes of the autobahn were channelled towards the shores. That would certainly have caused us considerable delay. We lost a few minutes heaving one crashed car back on to the other lane. The lady driver was unhurt and profuse in her thanks, not appreciating that our aim was not truly philanthropic but rather to free up our own passage. On crossing the frontier into Germany, Roger alerted us to the fact that 5 pence pieces worked in Deutschmark machines dispensing ice cream and lemonade. He had armed himself with a small stock of these in preparation. He was to prove his worth frequently on the trip in securing good deals! As the sun rose higher, this proved a boon, brightening up our passage while Ian and I spent the time catching up on each other's news, as it was some time since our last get-together.

We stopped for splendid sausage and mustard sandwiches at a service station and there, for the first time, experienced the shock of high German petrol prices. It grew ever hotter, requiring more lemonade and making the arrival at 4.30 at our intended campsite at Barensee near Frankfurt all the more appealing. Here, there was a fair sized lake and the site was crowded with German Sunday trippers. Out we poured to survey the scene, while Donald worked at timings and distances. This was to be one of his obsessions each day, just as the daily diary was mine.

We decided against putting up the tents till the crowds dispersed, fearful lest our unfamiliarity with the procedure should make us look ridiculous. Few of us had been trained as scouts! Instead, we opted for bathing in the deep but none too clear water of the lake, before sprawling on our lilos around the grass. After 6.00, when the day trippers were largely dispersed, we set about erecting our tents. The biggest held four comfortably, though designed for five persons, and this was my billet along with Hillbill, Campbell and Douglas; another tent took three and two smaller ones each held two. Thus we were accommodated at the outset though all commented that space was tight in the tents. Needless to say, it did take some time to get the tents up and we were glad that the spectators were few. Our minibus served us both as a secure point and a store. There followed showers before a decent meal, comprising thick soup followed by sausage again, but with salad accompaniment and lashings of mineral water. After that, we sampled the excellent German beer before turning in. Campbell was mocked for his comment that Ausfahrt must be a major city, to judge from the many signs to it leading off the autobahn. But then, he had studied Classics at the High

School and was unfamiliar with German road signage!

Come Monday, we were up sharp at 7 am preparing for Austria. Hillbill was up much earlier thanks to a bout of sickness in the night. This occasioned his taking an early plunge in the lake before cleaning up around his bedding. Perhaps it was brought on by his formidable array of tablets - he was into stomach tablets twice daily and tablets to ward off the impact of the sun. Antimalarial tablets would soon be added to his daily dosage. In his hasty departure in the night, the tent flap got ripped. I was already a week into my antimalarial treatment and had started salt tablets that day, on observing that yesterday's heat and inactivity had resulted in swelling of the ankles. This was all part of acclimatising ourselves and we kept careful watch across the party right from the start. We breakfasted on rolls and hot coffee from our own store and then set about striking camp and loading up the roof rack. All this took till 9 am, when we were ready for off. We were confident that we would get slicker at the loading as we proceeded. Before we left, I treated myself to a shower - no queuing necessary unlike the previous night - and a carton of yoghurt. I set great store on the curative properties of yoghurt right from the outset!

On the two lane motorway, we struggled to pass a convoy of American army trucks, but no sooner had we succeeded than a petrol stop around 11.30 allowed them to seize the lead once again. Petrol again required a stop at 1.30 and this allowed us to draw on the kitty and refuel ourselves with the obligatory sausage and mustard. We swept past München (Munich) on an excellent ring road while most of the party slept. This was already proving a common feature on the longer runs: first games, next chat, thereafter sleep, usually resulting in amusing postures for the entertainment of those who contrived to stay awake. Our next stop was at the Austrian border where prices for food and fuel suddenly took a welcome drop. A full tank in Austria in these distant days cost £5.50, against £7.50 in Germany. The temperature was pretty steady at 80°F, though naturally this fell when we were travelling in higher ground. As with Germany, we found the frontier officials less than interested in stamping passports and several of us chose to walk across the border to ensure that the precious stamp was obtained! Austria seemed more colourful and fresher, though there appeared to be less traditional costume worn than I recalled on earlier visits. Interesting church steeples, lakes and window boxes festooned with flowers remained unaffected. It was fully 9 pm when we reached a Gasthaus near Bad Aussee on the road to Grundlsee. The proprietress had little difficulty persuading us to stay overnight, as the surroundings amid trees and hills were cool and quiet with a mountain stream flowing past. She served us an excellent traditional meal of soup, schnitzel and salad washed down with fine beer. With an eye to future trade, she also ensured that we took away her visiting cards and brochures. After a relaxing evening and a few songs – I had thought to bring song sheets from home to assist, as previous trips had shown that tunes were better known than words - we were all bedded down by midnight, with only three in the big tent, as Douglas was trying the van for size.

Tuesday saw us on the move by 7 am with the stream serving as a pleasant arouser. We had our own breakfast supply of rolls and coffee and left by 8.00, after taking our leave of our cheerful hostess. We paused in the town to buy up a few provisions for travel and then headed off for Graz. The road proved poor and the scenery deteriorated as we approached the Jugoslav border. After a glimpse of the trams in Graz, we crossed over to be admired and counted by the customs officers. The headlines indicated some currency reorganisation in Austria but we were unaffected and the exchange rate was much as we expected. Here, we had a pause for a light lunch and the opportunity to marvel at and mock Campbell's mottled tan effect resulting from a wide meshed T shirt. Then we headed off for Zagreb and Beograd (Belgrade) at the back of 2.00 in uncomfortably hot and humid conditions. The morning cool at 64°F had soared to its more usual 80°F by midday. We endeavoured to make our passage more bearable by a prolonged bout of cards, mainly solo. The so-called highway for Beograd (Belgrade) was poorly surfaced and our progress was further impeded by numerous ox-drawn farm carts. The appearance of a steam engine at a level crossing offered some compensation for further delay. Beograd proved beyond reach and we stopped at a camp by Slavonski Brod at 8.30 as darkness fell. This made locating the camp tricky and the erecting of our tents a mini nightmare. Showers were cold and the Tourist Restaurant on site was lamentable. Prices were high, insects were abundant and the food atrocious. Our goulash was a revolting mix of bone, gristle and fat. Meat was a rare find amid the offering! However, the bread was fresh and acceptable. We made our feelings clear and this brought about a substantial reduction in the final bill. We made for bed in high dudgeon around 11.00.

I spent a comfortable night but was wakened early by a French party leaving from beside our space. We bought a loaf to have with our marmalade and coffee and then presented ourselves at the office for payment. The boss appeared swiftly from nowhere and away we went at 8.15. Hillbill and I spent much of the morning making repairs to the torn front of our large tent to make it mosquito proof. We relied on close stitching and the insertion of some muslin under the tent flap, as well as a few pieces of plaster. This was as good as it would get! Nearing Beograd at 11.00, we had a petrol stop. Filling the tank with some 50 litres now cost £4, thanks to petrol coupons we had obtained in Britain. These were intended as an incentive for tourists to spend more time travelling in the country but we used them simply to lower our costs. Naturally, we all piled out at the garage to stretch our legs and bare our chests - going without shirts was becoming standard for most of us. It reduced the need for frequent washes of clothes! Again, we resorted to cards to pass the time and progressed from solo to Knockout whist and

Twist. *En route* Niş, we stopped for eggs, bread and fruits with wine and watched a group of locals engaged in an illegal gambling game. Earlier, we had tried to leave the highway and have lunch in a little village. But all we managed, thanks to language difficulties, was to attract a horde of curious peasants. So we proceeded to Niş where we were caught in a rainstorm, with streets awash and brown with mud. We paused to marvel at the nearby river in violent spate along with a Turkish American who was dining with his lady by the roadside. Such had been the storm that we worried if the roof had remained watertight, but all seemed well when we risked a quick survey.

Leaving Jugoslavia proved easy but entry into Bulgaria at Kalotina was slow, with queues of cars and then queues at banks and customs. Exchange rate favoured cash, as I discovered only too late. Scottish bank

Another day dawns and coffee beckons at Sofiya camp site

cheques got short shrift but Campbell scored when they paid him double in error - not that we were exchanging much anyway: £2 cheques were our standard. We had to take out £7 additional insurance for the passage of the vehicle through Bulgaria. All in all, over an hour was spent in banking, but customs showed a surprising lack of interest in us. They all but stripped a French car ahead of us in the queue and let us pass through with little more than a glance. It was again dark when we reached the campsite near Sofia. The ground here was soaking and the site rather primitive. Still, the tents were put up with only a little difficulty and we rushed away to have meatballs served at tables covered with fresh new cloths in a shabby verandah, roofed rather like a railway station. A policeman was on duty. His job seemed to be keeping back the locals who were drinking at tables all around. Bolstered by the cheapness of the food, we progressed to pork steak followed by cheese and washed down by a decent wine. The night went on late.

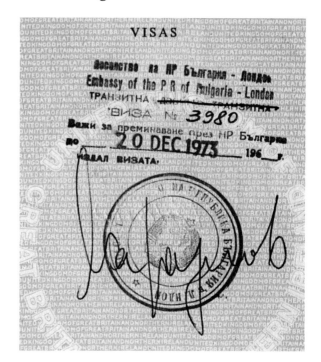

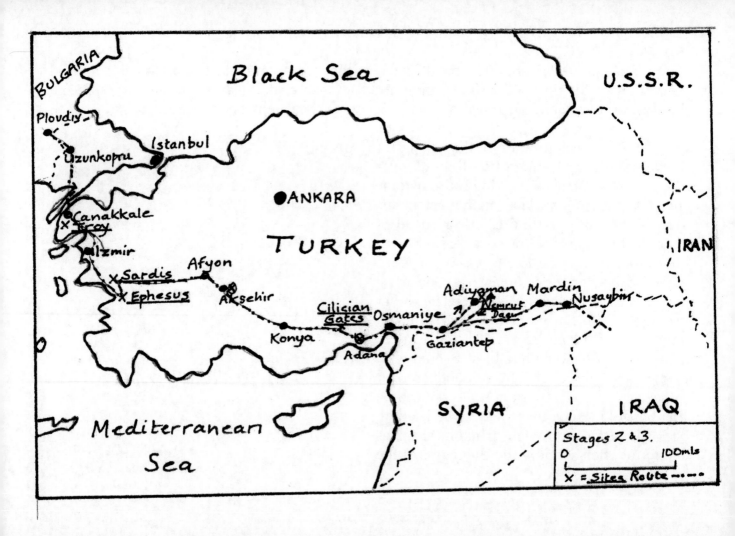

Stage 2

Thursday 5 July - Monday 9 July

Bulgaria into Turkey; through the Cilician Gates

Today, we rose near 8 am and freshened up with showers. Payment took ages and it was after 9 when we hit the road. I started my Nivaquin treatment against malaria today with no noticeable side effects. The morning was largely taken up with cards and chess, leading to a lunch stop at midday. Again, we were into sausage and salad, though Ian and

I indulged in some of my mother's trusted Durham Apple cake - this was a staple item on most of my foreign trips - and a modicum of wine for good measure. Increasingly, we were convincing ourselves of the curative properties of wine as well as yoghurt! En route Plovdiv over a mountain pass, a stone thrown up by a passing car smashed the windscreen. This was serious and necessitated use of our temporary screen till a permanent repair could be effected. Luckily, we had made provision for such a contingency when we were planning the trip! The screen was fitted in a dry period between showers, but when we continued on our way the clouds burst and there was a good going thunderstorm. The screen coped admirably to our great relief. It was rather early in the trip to face up to a serious problem.

Our next stop, after crunching along some poor roads, was the frontier. In Bulgaria, we

Attracting local interest as we prepare to leave Uzunköprü

were subjected to little more than a friendly smile and no delay. However, the Turks were changing shifts and this meant a long wait. Darkness was falling when we got under way again, after a brief call at the bank and a cursory check by the Turks. Arrival at Edirne, a sizeable town with some important sights for travellers with time in hand unlike ourselves, was cue for a brief meal stop and we celebrated with rice soup and chicken. From there, we left the Istanbul road and headed for Uzunköprü where we planned to stop overnight, as it was getting late. We inspected two hotels there and chose the slightly superior one, distributing our party into groups of five, four and two at competitive rates - little more than 25 pence a person. Admittedly, the rooms could hardly be called clean, but we were little better after all our travels. As often, the toilets were the worst feature and there were no showers. As it was near 2 am when we got ensconced, little time was wasted in bedding down.

We were stirring by 8.30 and the heat was fast rising. In fact, it reached 90F today and was still extremely humid. Despite our fears and expectations, none of us encountered a mosquito in the night. So far, only Roger could claim a visible bite. This he got while snacking at Edirne when some adventurous insect, probably an ant, invaded his trouser leg. We roamed the streets in quest of stamps to send cards home but were unsuccessful. So we consoled ourselves with chocolate pudding followed by Turkish tea. Once we had paid the hotel, loaded the roof rack, drawn money and made our way through throngs of wondering children and adults, we set off at the back of 10.00. The military official on duty, whistling aimlessly at traffic, was no doubt glad to see us go and the children disperse. We drove to the Sea of Marmaris at Eçeabat, where we caught the car ferry across the Dardanelles for Çanakkale just as she prepared to cross over to

Our ferry to the East awaits at Eçeabat

the East. As it was now 2.30, we took lunch at Şehir Restaurant, which I knew from previous visits. This fortified us for our visit to Troy.

This year we were asked to pay more at Troy for using a camera than for actually entering the site, but admission was half rate as it was Friday. This was a lucky break and not planned! No new work could be seen on site and indeed the megaron or main palace was fenced off, as it was crumbling in part. Though it was already familiar to me and one or two others and not strictly within our project, we could not pass the rather disappointing and confusing site without a call. The younger lads had to see it, considering its fame in history and literature. Anyway, the location for Homer's *Iliad* and the war at Troy could hardly be bypassed by me as Classics adviser! The Persian king Xerxes and Alexander the Great had also stopped here in the course of their marches to offer sacrifice at the temple of Athene. Further, two of our number, Alasdair in particular, were also battle enthusiasts. The view across the plain from the hill was sufficient justification and the enormous trenches dug by Schliemann were impressive if unfortunate. Outside the site were the usual vendors selling every kind of tat imaginable. Wooden horses were of course plentiful!

Roger's account is rather disparaging with regard to Troy - perhaps I influenced him too much. He does admire aspects of Troy II such as the fortifications but regards the place overall as "a mess, many sites on top of one another" and "actually fairly small in area". Of course, such an accumulation of sites belonging to different periods is often a delight and challenge for archaeologists! Each to his own.

Under an hour sufficed for our visit before setting off, after a few quick drinks and much related discussion, for Altin camp

An impressive section of the city wall and tower at Troy VI

Trap for unwary tourists outside the walls of Troy

at Oren, by Edremit. We had been there the previous year and found it satisfactory. The same friendly girls with their Americanised English were in evidence to welcome us but no sign of the boss - Big Daddy, as we had previously named him. We had a welcome bathe at 8.30 as the sun set, before showering and having dinner. No mosquitoes were in evidence. Indeed, a fiery skinned Englishman roundly assured us that none existed here, though we remained unconvinced. The fixed meal was a bit disappointing though it filled a gap. Hillbill and I elected to have extra sweet to make us feel better. The site appeared markedly quieter than last year and the owner must have welcomed our trade. There were mighty "July bugs" whirring around, allegedly not dangerous but certainly alarming. One or two managed to get enmeshed in Greenock George's long fair hair and this caused a minor panic. Grasshoppers too were numerous but caused less concern than the buzz bombs. Roger was determined that we go to the disco and we obliged. There we were met by the family owners, including the boss, who recognised some of us from last year. Thereafter, we drifted off to bed after a singsong, hoping for a bug free night.

Saturday saw us up at 8.00 for a swim and wash and the opportunity of replenishing our water supplies. We took our leave of the camp owners - the boss ceremoniously shook my hand - and headed for Izmir where we hoped to fit a new screen. En route, I spotted a modern villa closely modelled on a Roman one such as Chedworth back in Gloucestershire, even to the portico. On the outskirts of Izmir, we came upon a shop selling windscreens and paid around £20 to have one fitted in 12 minutes flat, though this happened only once the boss was summoned and appeared in his Volkswagen. We chose the superior model

Fitting a new windscreen at Izmir while Donald looks on attentively

rather than a plain glass job. In our brief stop, a cheery and opportunistic little Turk in vest and apron by name of Mustafa dragged us over the road for a quick cup of tea. Several of us surprised him by not taking sugar, the norm in Turkey. Izmir, ancient Smyrna, looks out over the Aegean Sea and is a large, imposing city with many monuments. Our timetable ruled out a pause for sightseeing. It was after 2.00 when we rejoined the road for Efes or Ephesus, much the better for the fitting of a secure screen. This visit to Efes entailed a slight diversion but the site ranks among Turkey's finest.

At Efes, we drove up to the Magnesia Gate at 3.30, where Ian and I elected to clamber up and follow the city wall, sandal clad and soaked in sun oil. The walls follow the ridge of Mount Coressus and date to 3rd century BC. They are impressive though ruinous, with square turrets and occasional stairways to the parapet walk. We found little traces of other gates. This diversion took us about two hours and was hard going. We accumulated a good show of scars, scrapes and thorns. The rest were able to roam the excellent site and view the theatre, marble roads and numerous buildings. Ian and I had seen these previously and it is a marvellous site, well maintained and deservedly popular. Both of us were rather shaky after our efforts and the heat of the sun, but a quick call first at the beach and then the camp for water and salt tablets worked wonders. Pamuçak, at no great distance from Efes, boasted a new campsite with attractive shore. Here we did a small wash - shirts and handkerchiefs - before sunbathing for an hour. Then we went to the restaurant at sunset and feasted well. Most of the company there were Turks and they appeared to find the television quite fascinating, although in truth the quality was pretty awful in our estimation. We turned

Efes: agora and theatre seen from the Hellenistic wall on Mount Coressus

Efes: restored temple of Hadrian on the Marble Road

in early at 10.30 and found the heat fierce, not helped by anti insect cream, mosquito netting and the like.

Over the meal, there were ugly murmurs about missing out Sardis from the itinerary and choosing an easier and more direct route, rather than backtracking through Izmir. These I resisted. After all, we had embarked on a Persian journey and the renowned Persian Royal Road had its terminus at Sardis. Then, hadn't the Athenians burned it in 499 BC, thus causing Darius to invade Greece? Nor should we forget that, before falling before the army of the Persian Cyrus the Great, Sardis had been capital of Lydia, whose king Croesus was reckoned wealthiest of mankind, giving rise to our description "as rich as Croesus." Alexander too showed favour to Sardis after defeating the Persians at Granicus in 334 BC. It could not be bypassed!

After a fitful and uncomfortable sleep, owing largely to the presence of plenty mosquitoes, a morning dip was welcome. It would almost certainly be our last sea bathe for a long time! The camp site was close to swamp and marshy ground which explained the abundance of mosquitoes eager to feed on us. After coffee and with the insects already pestering, we left sharp at 8.15 on Sunday morning with Sardis (Turkish Sart) our goal. Donald navigated us impressively through Izmir and our finances ruled out breakfast. The windscreen had depleted the kitty and banks were shut. Weekends were always tricky when it came to finding cash! We reached Sardis soon after 11.00, with not another tourist to be seen. The modern village is small, betraying nothing of its historical significance as is the case too, I suppose, with Troy or Ephesus. Our first call was at the massive Hellenistic temple of Artemis, the most impressive remains on the

Sardis: temple of Artemis

Sardis: restoration of Roman gymnasium and synagogue complex

site. What a contrast with the famed Temple of Artemis at Ephesus where little more than the overgrown site survives today! An immediate task was to dissuade David from a desire to climb the acropolis. This would have been a hard grind and time consuming. We contented ourselves with a look at the gymnasium, where major reconstruction work was being done, and the line of the Royal Road, mainly in its Roman upgrade.

This was another of Darius' great achievements, when he reorganised road links across his empire. The road ran for some 1600 miles from Sardis to Susa through the Cilician Gates, Nineveh and Babylon, with an extension to Persepolis. Mounted couriers could traverse its course in 7 days according to the Greek Herodotus, that marvellous historian and raconteur. He records in Book 8 of his Histories that such was the design of the road and its stages that nothing was faster than these couriers nor could check their progress, be it snow, rain, heat or darkness. Alexander the Great used the Royal Road to invade Persia, the Romans reconstructed it and we too were to put it to good use. The river Pactolus at Sardis was a dry bed, so there was no gold to be expected there despite its reputation in ancient times for carrying gold dust from its source! A rash of youngsters snooped around the fields offering coins and ceramics, unseen by the elderly site custodian who presented us with the Visitors' book to sign as we prepared to head off.

We had a roadside stop for a scanty lunch about 1.00 and amused ourselves watching a tour bus driver cleaning out his coach. The lesson was not entirely lost on us! Our road to Afyon followed the line of the Royal Road, passing through barren countryside with extinct volcanoes and lava flows before opening out into a fertile plain. At the outskirts of Afyon, we passed along a line of light standards suited for dual carriageway. The only problem was that the carriageway was single and so one lamp fitment was left unfilled all along the line! Afyon was reached by 5.00 and the towering acropolis could not fail to impress. Several tour buses were sitting in the main street, an indication of the town's attractions. Interestingly, its full name in Turkish means "Black Castle of Opium" but I doubt this was one of the attractions! We drove on with a brief stop for Turkish tea at a village where our shirtless state drew comment.

During the drive today, we were frequently flagged down by local Turks who took us for dolmuş or taxis. These are invariably minibuses running between towns and villages and so we looked the part in our bus! Like us, they often have substantial loads, sometimes even livestock, carried on their roofs. Tortoises were often seen along the road. We encountered several huge stretches of road under construction and the dust got everywhere, inside as well as outside. Akşehir was reached before 8.00 and we immediately started a search for hotels. After some misunderstandings, we settled for about forty pence a head, an intermediate price. The hotel was clean with bath but no showers. We were also presented with keys, a rare accessory! Donald and co-driver Bill (Billco) drew the short straw with a windowless room but it was quieter too. Finding decent eating places in this small town proved difficult and we split up. My group was lucky and had a first rate stew followed by a strong yoghurt and quaffable wine. We sampled a raki before trying out the town cinema at 11.00. This proved primitive with obvious reel changes and fake scenes but interesting for all that.

We shared the room overnight with a few beetles but no other bugs. I was up by 7.30

on Monday and used room telephones to rouse some of the party who were in deep slumber. Greenock George was especially hard to rouse and required beaters outside his door. We were spread out all over the hotel! A bank visit was now essential and we hit the street. Light drinks were hard to find - probably as this was an area rarely visited by tourists - so we settled for a pricy çay (Turkish tea) at the hotel. The boss gave us a couple of posters advertising a local festival for Nasreddin Hoca, pictured as a local joker on a mule. This festival ended on the 10th and was celebrated annually. Apparently he was a philosopher and sage noted for his jokes and anecdotes and Akşehir was the place he lived and died away back in the 13th century. We also borrowed a brush and shovel to give the bus a good clean inside - as you see, the lesson from the previous day was not lost on us - before filling up the tank with 53 litres of Turk Petrol at the local garage for under £3. Then, it was off across the barren steppes of the Konya plain.

Konya, a large and historic city, stands nearly 3,500 feet above sea level. In recognition of its significance, it boasted at least six banks and we arrived there ahead of noon closing. Much walking was involved and the usual long queues. Four of us changed money before we drove off across the continuing barren plain. Regrettably, we had not time to see its famed monastery of the Dancing Dervishes. As we drove, we saw plenty peasants cutting the wheat with scythes and sickles. A few had threshing machines which, though primitive, appeared effective in separating seed from chaff. Several wells with high water poles were another feature. Large water channels, almost like canals, also were seen enclosed by high clay dykes. Herds of goats appeared intermittently and

Poster showing Nasreddin Hoca, philosopher and wit, presented to us at Akşehir

the ground looked very white. We failed to work out why this should be the case, though salt or limestone was proposed. Dust was blowing in the strong wind. Water was clearly in short supply. As we headed for the Taurus Mountains and the famed Cilician Gates, we were faced with some 25 kilometres of road under construction, with resulting dust and bumps. En route Ereğli, we diverted to see the volcanic crater lake of Karapinar for a photo stop. The water was deep blue/green and we were watched here with interest by what was probably a jerboa or desert rat. Presumably, visitors of our appearance were a rare sight! As we left the lake, we had a fine view of a couple of steam engines chuffing their way across the vast plain towards Ulukişla. This town, taking its name from a 17th century caravanserai, was seen as a good excuse by us for a brief stop to take a late brunch. Some of us set off in quest of medicinal yoghurt and were rewarded by an accompaniment of fresh, warm bread.

Here the scenery took a turn for the better and we stopped again to photograph the Taurus Mountains. Plenty snow covered the upper slopes at some 8 or 9,000 feet. We were currently crossing a high level plain at around 3,500 feet. Soon we were dropping steeply towards the Cilician Gates with the gorge of the River Cydnus appearing on alternate sides of the road. Much of the road here was new, with work still continuing. Traffic was horrendous. There was a truly incredible flow of trucks climbing up from the coast and heading probably for Ankara and beyond. A lot of the vehicles were Bulgarian. The views were spectacular, though the ancient rock cut inscription at the actual Gates was a sad affair and badly worn and defaced. We risked our necks parking precariously at the road edge, as no parking area was provided. After all, we

Heavy traffic at the Cilician Gates and gorge of River Cydnus on the Royal Road

had to get up close to the ancient inscription and jay walking was second nature to most of us hailing from Glasgow! Nonetheless, this proved quite a challenge.

From here we climbed zig zag down to Tarsus, braving oncoming lorries at several sharp bends. Donald performed immaculately! It was 6.30 when we eventually joined the Tarsus/Adana road and soon we crossed Hadrian's bridge, restored later by Justinian, into Adana, a prominent and prosperous city. Here we were shocked when we had a look at the hotels on offer on our terms. They were thoroughly disreputable, even by our standards. But we were lucky to find a Mocamp on the outskirts and the overnight bill was little more than £5 for vehicle and tents. The site was well maintained and provided showers. With the humidity being awful and after a long haul over dusty roads, we thought these heaven sent.

Thoroughly refreshed by showers, we started to consider sustenance, which had been sadly lacking over the day. No wine was available at the Mocamp restaurant and this we valued for its medicinal qualities. Thus we were provided with an excuse to make for town and the camp boss was happy with this idea, as he was embroiled in an argument over a bill with an Englishman. Six of the party decided to be bold and take a taxi into town while Donald, Billco and the three Glens lads stayed at camp. We were whisked into town at near enough 100 kilometres an hour to get the adrenalin flowing! Our first call was for a delicious lemony soup. Then we moved on to a second restaurant for omelette and salad, with wine brought in from outside. We were located one storey up, with a fan roaring overhead. Now feeling satisfied and having bought a heap of grapes at a roadside vendor, we hailed a smallish Fiat taxi and all six piled in to share the experience and test its capacity. We met the rest making for bed in the camp after 11.00 and satisfied ourselves that we had made the right choice on hearing what had been on offer. The humidity both in and out our tents prepared us for a less than comfortable night.

Entry (at Edirne) and exit
(at Nusaybin) from Turkey

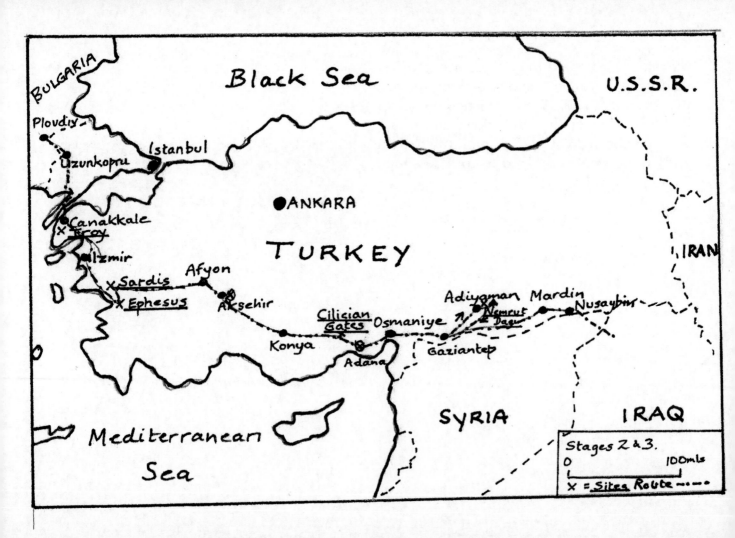

BULGARIA

Black Sea

U.S.S.R.

Ploudiy

Uzunkopru

Istanbul

●ANKARA

TURKEY

IRAN

Canakkale
X Troy

Izmir

X Sardis   Afyon

X Ephesus

Aksehir

Cilician
Gates

Osmaniye

Adiyaman Mardin

Nemrut   Nusaybin
Dagi

Konya

Adana

Gaziantep

SYRIA

IRAQ

Mediterranean

Sea

Stages 2 & 3.

0   100mls

X = Sites Route ----

Stage 3

Tuesday 10 July - Friday 13 July

Conquest of Nemrut Dağı; through Gaziantep; past the Euphrates to the Turkish frontier

Campbell and I had a terrible sleep and we were soaked with perspiration. Our last hour from 5.30 am was the best, when I risked insects and opened the tent flap - we were paranoiac about supposed mosquitoes waiting outside to get us! The shower was a joy, as was the calming coffee. Donald and Billco also had a shocking night. We left at 8.00 and had a thirty minute pause on a climb up the flank of Mount Amanus after passing through Osmaniye, while Billco investigated trouble with the carburettor. The engine was overheating. He reckoned poor quality petrol could be the problem and reduced the petrol flow. It was a real boon having someone who understood the workings of engines! We brewed tea during the stop and were objects of fascination for passing lorry drivers as we supped and sunbathed. We descended to the plain near Gaziantep where we were met by a splendid, new, broad road. The numerous bends could be forgiven!

Soon we left the main road and made for Turkoğlu and Maraş. In the former, we were sent on a deviation through the back streets and across a dried river bed, since the army was in action repairing a damaged bridge.

Our bus (left) boils as we climb up from Osmaniye - note the local dolmuş, centre

Delays here gave the local kids a bean feast, as they banged our sides and clambered over us like monkeys, until a shop owner came to our rescue and sent them on their way. Maraş was a lunch stop - it had little else to offer - and we split up. As usual, Ian and I went in quest of yoghurt and soup with ice cream to follow. While waiting for our drivers to return, we took shelter from the usual mob of staring children in a teashop. Next came a prolonged delay while jerry cans were filled. Leaking lids encouraged locals to offer polythene covers to tighten the screw top but this was not much of a success and we opted for keeping them upright. Throughout this palaver, Donald sat patiently in the bus - wise man! There was a torrid wind whistling through Maraş and the temperature in the bus was over 90F.

Arrival at Adiyaman brought fresh worries, as the differential in the bus sounded increasingly unhealthy, particularly when we were driving along unsurfaced roads. Our plan had been to take a diversion from our route so as to visit the spectacular mountain site at Nemrut Dağı. A call at the local tourist office caused us to rethink. They declared that a jeep was required - though this would be needed only if we were not intending to climb from the base. Here we had a new challenge! We had intended to take our bus to Eski Kahta, a little village at the mountain foot, boasting its own fairly well preserved mediaeval castle. The differential worry required a change of plan, though we seriously considered taking the risk and driving up to the village! Sanity prevailed: Donald and Billco would head for Malatya for repairs, as we had been told there was a good garage there. The rest of the party picked up essentials, along with bread, grapes, water and wine and piled into a dolmuş or taxi. The cost for this plus a guide worked out near £30 a head. We rejected the

Looking up to the summit of Nemrut Daği, all 7,500 feet of it

offers of jeeps at a higher rate despite their ability to take us up close to the summit. We had to prove ourselves and climb some 7,500 feet to the important site, created towards the end of the 1st century BC by king Antiochus I of Commagene who claimed descent from one of Alexander the Great's generals.

This abandonment of the bus might seem audacious but was nothing when compared with our previous year's trip to Syria and Jordan. On that occasion, you may recall, the ill starred Land Rover, after a few incidents, broke down completely at Damascus, leaving those of us who were determined to carry on to see rose red Petra and Jerash, as per travel plan, with a hard decision. In the end, the party broke up and half of us proceeded, using public transport and taxis, to accomplish our tour while the remainder stayed with the bus till it was repaired. We all met up four days later in Beirut, after many adventures.

By comparison, the detour to Nemrut Dağı seemed a dawdle!

On leaving around 8.00 pm, our taxi driver fooled about with various unnecessary stops to suit himself and his personal requirements and picked up a few of his mates. Time seemed to be of no consequence. He then appeared to get lost, before meeting up with two French lads in a Peugeot who were on the same mission as ourselves. Perhaps, on reflection, he was deliberately wasting time so as to join up with this other group. They also had the route guide with them. He pursued a wild course on desperate roads in the darkness and succeeded in getting us all jumpy and irritated, with the Peugeot party driving at our back. It was 10.00 when we arrived at Eski Kahta in the mountains. The plan had been to camp down at the school as directed by the guide but, on lighting a fire in the moonlight, we discovered the school grounds were alive with ants, so this was not acceptable. The toilet proved to be a blacked out hut, with water to be found at a well in the village square. Next, the guide suggested sleeping overnight in the actual school but this proved to be locked and the schoolmaster absent on a visit. We took a snack by our fire and pondered, until the guide suggested that we should sleep on his roof, made of clay and pounded stone but mercifully quite flat. The house was without water or electricity. Beggars can't be choosers and so we accepted the proposal. The roof swayed and shook alarmingly as we trooped across it, the two French lads included. We drank our wine and enjoyed our meagre rations before bedding down at midnight on our lilos under a magnificent canopy of stars. The rest of the family were also sleeping up on the roof. The high wind shrieked around us and I scratched my two recently acquired bites on my ankles until I fell asleep.

Wednesday was to be our attack on the site. The party was up by 4.00 am and we all slept reasonably, if briefly. We were accompanied by a mule carrying water and provisions - this was one advantage of having a guide! Also in the party were the two French lads, the guide and a friendly dog. We set off up a stream of clear, delicious water following a clearly marked mountain track. After an hour and a half of steady and fast walking, we reached Hokim village. Here, the guide called on his local contacts and led us into a mud floor hut where we doffed our shoes and sprawled on rugs and cushions while being served Ayran (similar to buttermilk) as well as tea and water.

After an hour had passed, we resumed our march upwards at 7.00 and there the party began to find its own pace. The two Frenchies took the lead at first, till Greenock George and I overtook the slower. George was next to fall back a little and I kept pace with Jacques, the

Head of Antiochus on the West Terrace

Fallen heads from the mighty statues on the West terrace - another party visits the site from a vehicle

The West Terrace seen from above

Roger features as a latter day Prometheus spread-eagled on the summit

more lithe and faster French chap, till cramp took him out the running for being first at the top and we stayed together. As we were in the lead, we drifted off the course and clambered up shale and then porous limestone rocks which chafed my fingers. So we struggled to the summit, ignoring the jeep track and restaurant, and arrived there at 8.40 am. After a short time, George and Roger showed up and Roger spread-eagled himself on the summit mound like a latter day Prometheus awaiting the arrival of the vulture to rip out his vital organs. Then came the second French lad with the faithful mule in attendance and not long after came Ian with the heel of his sandal fixed with tape. Campbell and Hillbill completed the group, as the three lads from Glens were at the tail and got no further than the restaurant. I had expected David at least to make the top, recalling his wish to climb the acropolis at Sardis, but perhaps lack of sleep was taking its toll.

The tumulus mound marked the summit and on either side below it were the East and West terraces. These were of similar design but with a great altar on the East terrace. Inscriptions revealed that Antiochus I of Commagene, 69-34 BC, was buried here and his final resting place showed him in the company of the deities Fortuna Commagene, Zeus, Apollo/Mithras and Herakles/Ares. The gods, Antiochus naturally included, sat on immense thrones flanked by stone eagles and lions. Over the years, these mighty images have fallen and present an impressive array of heads for the visitor to study. Antiochus claimed descent from both Alexander the Great and Darius of Persia and had no small conceit of his importance. We were told that the Fortuna figure on the East terrace was the last to fall, struck by lightning. Some sculptured stones were dark sandstone and others limestone, brought up from a place

Déjà vu: here we look down on the East Terrace with its altar

some hours distant - so the guide informed us. After the conquest, we indulged in an omelette at the restaurant and served with hard scones. Then it was back downhill and the guide directed us to a zig zag steep descent, with the three Glens lads in the rear and the guide to keep them together.

The advance party on the descent was Jacques, Ian, George, Roger and myself and we were back at the river meeting point at 1.30. There we were joined by Bill with the other French lad and next came - horrors! - the guide on the mule. No sign of the Glens trio nor of Campbell. The guide admitted that he had gone ahead and so agreed to go back to locate them. We had told the dolmuş driver to expect us around 2.00. While the minutes sped past, we drank water copiously and munched raisins and plums supplied by interested locals. At 4.30 the wanderers appeared, weary and sun scorched after some 12 hours exposure on the hill. Campbell had taken a tumble on the shale during his descent and suffered a bruised leg and cut lip. This helped to explain the delay. We had little time to dally before the dolmuş driver picked us up and drove over the mountains to Adiyaman. At one very steep incline, we all had to get out the vehicle and allow it to struggle up empty. I insisted on a quick stop to view and photograph Severus' bridge over the River Nymphaeus dating to 196 AD. It was splendid though isolated and hard to snap. I took a view including the driver as a negotiating tool. We were 3 hours late leaving Eski Kahta and, by assuring the driver that I would get him a copy, we were able to get the extra time written off! I gave the guide a tip but refused his request for extra cash for the mule, as this was not in our original contract.

At Adiyaman, we took our leave of the French lads and were delighted to find

Roman bridge over the River Nymphaeus

Gaziantep from the fortress - quite a contrast in the buildings

63

Donald and Bill waiting as arranged, though mystified by our apparent disregard for timings. The differential still defied treatment and we had no option but to proceed. In semi darkness, we left for Gaziantep after a brief delay while we secured soup and yoghurt to keep body and soul together. The climbing party was shattered, so that two road checks by soldiers were barely noticed as we made the four hour trip to Gaziantep. Midnight was passed before we got there and there followed a half hearted hotel search. We were lucky and secured a nice set of clean and quite fragrant rooms at 30 pence a person. There were, however, no showers to be had. Tired though we were, a few of us went out in quest of some sustenance before turning in.

If Thursday 12th was glorious, it was because we had a day of comparative rest. Donald and Billco wanted to try again and effect repair to the differential if this proved necessary, but once again they were doomed to failure. The party, however, welcomed the break. Gaziantep has a long and distinguished history but was not really within the scope of our project. Still, the stop allowed us a chance to look around the modern city a little. Bank visits were made and a substantial breakfast enjoyed at leisure. Again, I enjoyed the local Ayran and trusted that it would have the same medicinal effects as I hoped for with wine. George and Alasdair were the first of the group to go down with a stomach bug here with all the concomitant misery, requiring hasty toilet calls. We blamed exposure to the sun but feared that the affliction could become widespread if this were indeed the cause! We were too late to visit the museum in the morning and had to wait for afternoon opening. To pass the time, Ian, Roger and I made a steep and dusty assault on the castle through a break in the encircling barbed wire. The impressive and extensive castle evidently was first developed by Justinian in 6th century AD and additions had been made over successive years. The castle was theoretically closed but unofficially occupied, as the detritus around the buildings clearly showed. From the castle, we patrolled the lower streets around the market and watched a traffic policeman kicking a Turk who had made the mistake of jeering at us. Foreigners clearly counted for something in Gaziantep! At 3.30, we went to the museum and paid half rate. There was a lot to be seen, but labelling was largely in Turkish and dating hard to determine. There were fine coins and cylindrical seals. Various periods were represented such as Hittite, Syrian and Assyrian. There was also an open air display but labelling again was a problem for us. I used the toilet facilities in the museum to clean off the dust from the castle!

Back at the hotel, we rested before checking on the party's general health. Our lavish, western use of toilet paper completely blocked up the toilets in the hotel. Only "squatters" were available and no ceramic bowls. Donald was sharing his bed with a persistent flea and had no success in tracking it down. In the evening, we all went out for dinner and found for ourselves a lovely strong, peppery soup followed by omelette served in the pan. The meal was well priced. I then went off with Ian for the ritual wine and yoghurt plus, quite unusually, kebabs. It is surprising how little meat we risked trying. Cost could have been a factor and our gristly experience in Jugoslavia! We successfully sent cards home from Gaziantep. Stamp charges varied widely during the trip: 1.75 lira, 2.5 and 3.25 were charged at different times. George and Roger determined to try their luck at a night club. They found it poorly patronised and, confronted by several stout ladies, they fled instead to the cinema. Most of us were in bed by 11.00 at the hotel.

River Euphrates at Bireçik with ruins of a Crusader castle

Mardin lying below its Byzantine citadel

Friday saw us up by 7.00 and delighted to find water pressure was high. Last night it was variable and sometimes there was no water at all. So we felt properly clean for a change. My day started on a high with the execution of the flea which I caught in Donald's room. Of course, it had made him suffer over night and catching it now was rather too late to help! Still, it offered some sort of satisfaction! Billco had a disturbed night too, thanks to the inevitable stomach trouble. George and Alasdair had almost recovered from their bout. I had slight rumblings but hoped for improvement. Breakfast consisted of yoghurt, sweet melon and tea, before we headed off at 8.00. Petrol was dangerously low but after some worries we came upon a Super Mobil garage at Nizip and filled the tank. There ensued a long, hard, hot day with a stop for lunch in a roadside restaurant after 1.00. Extremely spicy onions were served with kebabs and plenty iced water. We immediately attracted the usual gathering of curious onlookers, Arabs, Turks and Kurds. We stopped at a bridge below Bireçik to cross the River Euphrates and enjoyed the diversion. A ruined fortress commanded the crossing. Then we resumed our route, playing solo again. Hillbill was feeling poorly, with headache and occasional nose bleeding.

A crossroads presented a problem: should we travel by Mardin or make for Nusaybin and cross a small piece of Syria? We chose Mardin as closer, with the intention of making further enquiries about the best approach to Mosul in Iraq. This presented us with a steep climb up to 4,000 feet in searing heat. The city was attractive, with a significant history and prominent citadel, but, as ever, our project did not permit a delay. We were immediately surrounded by children and curious onlookers, many wearing fine leather coats, despite the heat. After a struggle through the throng, we managed to locate a police station and found an officer with a smattering of English. He accompanied us back to the bus - thus clearing a passage for us as he did so - and studied our maps. It was decided to head rather for Nusaybin and the Syrian prospect.

We bounced along some 30 kilometres of unsurfaced road which made us all suffer, vehicle included. Army trucks too kept appearing, throwing up large stones and putting us into a state of alarm for the windscreen as we lurched along. One windscreen calamity was surely enough! At 6.30, we reached the Turkish frontier at Nusaybin, after driving along parallel to the frontier wires for most of those unpleasant 30 kilometres. Here, we were positively thrilled to find a first class tourist hotel, with plenty water and showers into the bargain. We could even wash travel stained clothes. Heaven!

The rooms too were excellent and a friendly Iraqi was waiting for us when cleaning was over. He took us to his restaurant where we enjoyed plenty bread and soup along with yoghurt, water and wine. Occasional nose bleeds prevented Hillbill from leaving the hotel, but none of us were for staying out late after our demanding day. Anyway, the town seemed quite dead, with unsurfaced streets to match the highway which we had experienced and rubble piled in the streets. I suppose the proximity of the frontier was the reason.

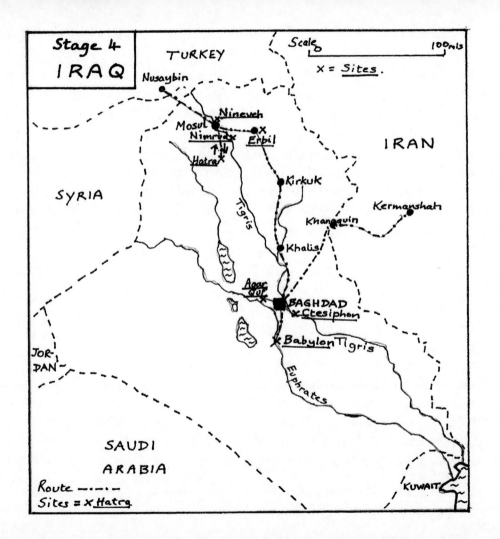

Stage 4

Saturday 14 July - Tuesday 17 July

Into Iraq via Syria; Mosul and a glimpse of the Assyrians and Parthians; arrival at Baghdad on the Tigris

We rose at 7.15 the following morning, after several of us had spent a fairly active night with toilet visits. Both Ian and I had by now joined other sufferers. Our wash on the roof dried completely and the total bill was under £4 for the whole party. As we paid, the rather grim looking boss passed the time killing flies on the windows and cleaning up the glass. We took last minute precautions before venturing out for breakfast, attracting the usual crowd of curious locals. After a modest breakfast, a few of us chose to walk along to the frontier post while the bus rolled up behind with a full tank. The border crossing took no more than forty minutes and the Turkish officers were friendly and attentive, offering seats and cooled water. Naturally, I also availed myself of the rather awful office toilet while we waited. Progressing from there, we came to the Syrian frontier at Kameshli and paid a small sum for a visa. Then began the entering of names in the books. The officials made no reference to their extensive record books, rather to our surprise. It was stuffy and hot and I was feeling a bit off colour. Donald was called away at the conclusion to draw the required Syrian money at the bank for vehicle insurance and we hoped that was our visit over. So it proved and we were free to go after an hour. This was better than our wildest dreams and seemed to justify the decision to cross a small area of Syria rather than face a lengthy detour.

The road we crossed in Syria to reach the border with Iraq was short and passed through a fertile region known as the Bec de Canard. Throughout its length, this frontier zone between Turkey and Syria is disputed territory. We took only a couple of hours to cross this tiny fragment of Syria and the road was appalling and peppered with potholes. Tel Kotchek was the next frontier point and we spent our Syrian money on ice cream and soft drinks before leaving Syria to enter Iraq. Thus refreshed, we faced the frontier police and found them friendly. In this regard they differed from the lorry drivers, who showed absolutely no regard for foreign road users!

They dealt with us expeditiously and allowed us free access to their toilets and washing facilities, throwing in iced water for good measure. After forty minutes, we were sent on our way with a warm handshake. Just as we were leaving through the last gate, a tiny child came over and asked "you see Customs?" and scuttled off. No doubt his father was enjoying his siesta by this time.

At 1.30, we arrived at the Iraqi militarist frontier, which was very different, though very close. Soldiers were everywhere and they had bayonets fitted on their rifles. Their assorted footwear made clear that boots were not on army issue! We joined a slow moving queue through the frontier post right behind a group of six Belgians, also travelling on a Ford Transit but, unlike us, heavily sponsored for their trip. Bells and telephones rang non stop during our passage towards customs and we were watched by prisoners looking out at us

Mosul as seen from our hotel

Ramparts of Sennacherib at Nineveh

from jail windows - a little disquieting! We sat uncomfortably for an hour until soldiers returned with our passports. There followed a further half hour while notes were made about us, and our camera numbers were registered too. Nothing was said about imported currency or travellers' cheques. We were now set before another section where passports were studied and reference made to books of records. Ian's signature had been pasted into his passport at a jaunty angle and this excited attention. Our visa issued by Afghan Iraqi interests caused further interest and comment. Donald was again made to obtain insurance for the vehicle costing just over £1 and lasting seven days. I had to make a quick call at the toilet and would have loved to take a drink from their cooled water supply but my nerve failed me. Now the name checking began, looking at first names in mistake for surnames and consulting records. At last, all

was completed after two and a half hours. At the last stage, we were allowed to fill our water bottles.

Then we were on our way again. All the frontier roads had been abysmal and badly surfaced and so it was a pleasure to be on a good road at last. However, we were also confronted with occasional police checks on the road to Mosul. We reached Mosul before the sun went down and were met by many friendly and welcoming Iraqis, one of whom led us to his brother's hotel, as well as showing us an alternative. We eyed up the two and decided that the first was hot and a bit grubby and went for the alternative Beirut Hotel. The price was the same, 25 pence per person, for clean rooms with showers and fans. Only the very steep stairs gave us any worries, what with our luggage. The boss supplied us with water and tea to refresh us on arrival and suggested that we eat on the premises once we had washed and changed. This seemed sensible and we set about another clothes cleaning session. The spread at dinner proved excellent with salad, olives and a range of greens, leading on to excellent goulash with rice and abundant supplies of tea. While we ate, local Arabs in full gear watched us from the sidelines, trying not to be seen. We were obviously a real thrill. In our turn, we watched our Iraqi friend, who had brought us to the hotel, as he played with little metal pieces and slammed them down noisily on the table. We really felt in another world. On concluding the meal, we were plied with grape juice and orange tea. At this point, we decided to explore Mosul a little and walked down by the Tigris, admiring the riverboats and bright neon signs. The old pre-war, single deck buses were a treat. Everywhere, the people were terribly friendly, almost overwhelmingly so. On getting back to the hotel, we kept the fans going all night and certainly needed them.

A good sleep was followed by a good shower and at 8.00 we went out through the suq quarter in quest of the main bank, open Sundays. The transaction was lengthy and we could not fail to note the damage to the exchange rate done by the flotation of sterling. Mosul had an attractive old world feel about it and the River Tigris added to its appeal. On our return to the hotel, we bought various necessities for a decent breakfast, aided as ever by the attentive boss who also paid for most of the purchases at this stage. We would be charged at departure. Hillbill was last to return - he had got himself involved changing money in two different banks. We set out for nearby Nineveh about 11.00 but, despite its historical significance, we saw little more than a tell buried under a mosque, a cemetery and houses. The modern town was fast absorbing the ancient site. So on we drove for Nimrud, once capital of the Assyrian empire, after filling up the tank for £2 with a hand operated pump. Petrol was stored in great raised tanks. The countryside was barren and like a desert, with only occasional huts and flocks of sheep.

Nimrud was a huge site, with defences covering nearly 5 miles. Projecting towers lined the walls. It was after midday when we arrived and the heat was oppressive. Still, we had to do our best and up the ziggurat we went to get a view over the site. Ashurnasirpal's palace, occupied over several centuries from around 9th century BC, was under reconstruction, using newly prepared mud bricks and stone slabs. Metal rods were being employed to reinforce the reconstruction. Human headed, winged bulls guarded the palace gates. The finished building will be striking. The other buildings on site were inevitably less impressive, as the ancient mud bricks have crumbled. We noticed a great, deep well with a stone trough and various door lintels and steps. Cuneiform script was much in evidence and traces of wall painting. We also noticed some attempts being made to experiment with colouring plaques. We allowed over an hour at the site, though Donald and Billco stayed away, preferring the shade. We were advised by a custodian to seek out a section of restored wall at Nineveh and made a detour back. The reconstructed Nergal Gate was our reward, one of fifteen along the walls. It dated to Sennacherib and displayed again human headed, winged bulls.

In the afternoon, after a Pepsi pause, we left for Ashur (Assur). We had earmarked this as Assyria's first capital, with various palaces, a fine Ziggurat and a commanding position by the Tigris. First, we got ourselves lost, before joining an excellent new road signposted for Baghdad. Alas, it proved too new and appeared on none of our maps. No sign off for Ashur was shown, though we pushed on about

Entering the palace at Nimrud

Nimrud: making mud bricks for the reconstruction

100 kilometres. Realising that our quest was in vain and greatly disappointed, we turned back and took the marked route for Hatra as an alternative site. This was not on the original itinerary. Again, we travelled on a fine, new road (except where damaged at a wadi) to this important Parthian capital city associated with King Sanatruq. It had withstood Roman sieges in 2nd and 3rd centuries AD, the first under Trajan's command and the next led by Severus. We drove through the moat and earth covered ashlar walls with turrets, straight into the centre of the site. Leaving the bus, we entered the administrative precinct through the NE gateway and climbed on top of it for the view over to the central, restored temple and beyond to the next sanctuary wall, with two huge iwans (vaulted halls with the fourth side open) as well as vaulted galleries. One temple was to the sun god, another of Hellenistic design, and the massiveness of scale throughout the site was impressive. Numerous wells supplied the site with water and many statues, often headless and with their right hand raised in greeting or respect, represented princes and priests. They wore baggy trousers drawn in at the ankles with straps and their faces reminded me of the sharp features of Stuart kings in Scotland, like James I and VI. Perhaps I was getting home sick! Statues of Sanatruq and his two sons, dating to 1st century AD, stood in a chamber behind the sun temple. Hellenistic influences were to be seen in the buildings and occasional inscriptions. There was a lot of reconstruction in progress and our visit, though not planned, was well rewarded. I suppose we would have remained oblivious to Hatra's spendour had we managed to find our way to Ashur!

Again, we spent over an hour at the site though Donald and Bill chose to stay with the bus. It was near 7.00 when we left, hoping to

Hellenistic style temple at Hatra

Hatra: one of its seven Gates and one bold spirit aloft

be back in Mosul before total darkness. All of us were feeling pangs of hunger and thirst by this time. I was prepared to forget my queasy stomach in the circumstances. Dust was blowing in the hot wind and eddying up from time to time. Despite our intentions, the last stretch was covered in the dark and progress was made harder by meeting cars without lights. Water was turned off at the restaurant when we arrived and we resorted to tubs provided in advance for our ablutions. Much better than nothing! Our meal was a delight with kidney soup, goulash and rice followed by tea and olives. Total bill for the meal for all of us was under six shillings. We bedded down soon after 11.00 after a very satisfying day.

Water was flowing again on Monday when we rose before 7.00 and rushed to enjoy showers. I had slept well and we were all alike refreshed. We went out for rolls and bread to take with our own marmalade supply. We left Mosul just as a procession was beginning through town to celebrate the Republic established with the end of monarchy in 1958. Boldly, I risked a couple of photographs, though I had no idea if this was permissible. Nothing untoward happened! Again we met a police point. This seems a regular feature - we had two such checks yesterday. Ten minutes were spent filling in cards and using phonetic spelling. Our two Williams in the group caused some confusion, as first names seem to get priority, no doubt mistakenly! They find our nomenclature confusing, even as we do theirs. Roger had regularly been recorded as Koger on the trip - a name which stuck - but this time he appeared as Loger for variety! Several more checks followed, usually before and after any significant town on the route and their duration varied greatly. The final one at Baghdad was, surprisingly perhaps, far the briefest. The police were quite overshadowed

Republic Day march in Mosul

Broken bridge over River Zab near Erbil - the gang is out for photos

everywhere by the army and this may be their way of feeling wanted!

Erbil (ancient Arbela) proved a disappointment, as the ancient tell with ramparts was much obscured by modern buildings and these largely shacks and stalls. It was near here that Alexander the Great defeated Darius III, thus allowing him unopposed entry to Persia. Donald persuaded us to take a tea stop here in rather dilapidated surroundings and then we were off through police stops and arid countryside, battered by a scorching wind at the window. Head coverings were found a useful protection. On reaching Kirkuk, centre of the oil industry, we stopped for lunch. Here our shorts attracted less than the usual curiosity in a town. We had a general policy in Iraq of wearing shorts for travel and site visits, while reverting to longs for towns. Obviously, day travel through towns broke the code! The lunch on offer was chicken with stewed salad and leban, a form of Turkish ayran. This is a most thirst quenching yoghurt drink with added salt and a favourite of mine. The price for lunch proved to be outrageous and the food poor. Other than myself, there were few takers. The old town across the dry river bed looked interesting but time forbade investigation. On we went through the village of Khalis where the muezzin at the mosque was in good voice. We had a snack here, aided over prices by a passing Iraqi with a surprising command of English. The village was near an oasis. We pressed on through barren country and occasional salt pans, with the road steadily improving.

We reached Baghdad as the sun was sinking and the sight of red and silver double deck AEC buses amazed us. They were some 40 years old and well kept. One bus was advertising Bata. We started our

Tahrir Square in Baghdad with an assortment of buses

River Tigris in Baghdad

hunt at some seedy hotels along the banks of the Tigris before abandoning thoughts of a river view and finding a more up-class street. After much haggling, we settled on the clean, air conditioned Serchinar hotel at around ten shillings a person. This was more expensive than our usual choice but it was superior. Delicious, cool orange juice quickly won us over! There had been a rally day for the Republic as in Mosul and the streets suggested that the day had been wild. Women too had been in the mob. We were better off on the road! Roger reports that he heard of executions taking place among the celebrations. We later discovered that there had been an attempted coup to overthrow the administration earlier in the month but this had proved disastrous and was savagely crushed. Could this explain the executions? Anyway, Lady Luck had clearly travelled with us and kept us free from obstructions or worse! Perhaps too it explains the frequency of road checks which we experienced and the omnipresent militia.

We had plenty to occupy us on arrival. Unloading the bus proceeded apace and Hillbill, Ian and I seized a rare en suite room. The hotel floors were marble and spotless while the evening air was quite cold. The heat throbbing in the outer walls told us of the heat we had missed during the day. We set off to find a restaurant but found nothing to compare with the splendour of Mosul with its padded chairs and ornamented walls. We finally contented ourselves with a local place offering omelette, cold meat roll and greens served with pickled cucumber. Not terrific, but extremely cheap at less than twenty pence per head. Such wine shops as we saw were shut, but the rally continued noisily on TV with impassioned addresses to the nation. We retreated to bed at the back of 11.00.

Tuesday brought a scorcher in Baghdad, famed city of the caliphs. Sadly, our impression of the city failed to measure up to our expectations. Certainly, it was huge and populous and had the Tigris at its centre but it was the Iraq museum and, of course, the buses which made the greatest mark. We were up by 8.00 and took breakfast in the hotel after showers. There followed a hunt for banks. The national celebrations for the Republic thwarted us and we found them all closed. Buildings and buses were bedecked with flags and other ornaments. Ian and I set off for the museum through numerous army installations, only to discover that we were heading in the wrong direction. So we readily jumped on a double decker and enjoyed seeing the city from the front seat on the top deck, while blasted by the hot air and with the conductor seated fascinated at our backs. Soldiers directed vehicles to the far side of the road, well clear of the main government buildings. Again, I risked photographs, to the consternation of a soldier. He was relieved to see that it was only buses which were attracting my interest.

Suqs and general squalor detracted a little from the thrill of being in Baghdad. On arrival, we found the Iraq Museum made no charge owing to the national holiday. Inside, we were greeted by a wealth of gold items, finds from Ur and elsewhere, and Assyrian tablets. The collection was truly spectacular and was seen only by Campbell, Roger, Hillbill, Ian and me. George was off colour and stayed at the hotel. Roger too was feeling sick but determined to make the effort. The museum shop was closed for the holiday, though Campbell was mistaken for another guest and received a gift pack containing literature and picture cards. Buses were out in force on the streets - there must be hundreds of double deckers, as well as a few single deckers from Budapest. We crossed the Tigris searching for the Tourist office, only to find it also was closed. We should have guessed! The numerous arcades en route provided welcome shelter from the heat. The traffic police could not have been more friendly and helpful as we made our enquiries.

We had agreed to meet at the hotel for 3.00, and took another bus, single deck this time. On arrival at the hotel, we slaked our thirst with fresh lemon. George was still sleeping when we got back and we let him lie. The three Glens lads elected to head off for the Military museum and the rest of us made for Aqar Quf, about 20 miles away. We sought directions from a group of youths dancing in the street, all part of the holiday atmosphere. One even accompanied us for about a mile to set us on the right road for the site. A good tarmac road led us there and apparently a campsite was being prepared. The 180 foot Ziggurat was the main attraction, as the surrounding temple and palace were ruinous, little more than hills of dry mud. The storeyed tower with four faces, designed to get closer to heaven and the gods, was constructed of mud bricks, with layers of reed every so often for stability. The structure dated from 15th to 12th century BC. The upper section was much eroded but the mud bricks were clearly visible, as were the straw layers. Birds used the nooks and crannies provided, for shelter and nesting. The Iraqis were busy making mud and clay bricks to reconstruct the lower area with a projecting plinth leading to the palace and religious buildings. It was obvious that this would be a major task but the remains were massive and would repay proper attention. The grounds round about were laid out in small lawns for camping when the project is completed. Water was available at the hut on the site.

Reconstruction at base of Aqar Quf ziggurat

Aqar Quf: 15th Century ziggurat

Our trip to Aqar Quf took three hours there and back but the time was well spent. It was also as near as we have yet come to the Euphrates, Iraq's other great river. The road out was well surfaced but, alas, unsigned in English. This was exactly the same for poor old Ashur, which we had missed. Ashur, for all its significance, did not even appear on the Iraqi tourist map, though shown on a site plan in the Iraq Museum. Only Hatra combined good signposting and an excellent road. I suppose time will put this to rights.

We were back in good time for showers at the Serchinar Hotel and found George still abed and sleeping. The Glens lads failed in their mission, as the Military museum was shut. They regretted their decision to miss out on Aqar Quf. A few of us took a double decker into town and walked along Abu Nawas street beside the Tigris as the sun set, enjoying the sight of the locals crowding the streets and restaurants or walking on mud flats at the river. Certainly, it was squalid in some parts but very atmospheric. Huge Tigris river fish were being fried and barbecued along the river banks but we were too wary to take the bait. We returned to Tahrir Square, found a suitably disreputable restaurant for a meal and beside it a post office. We also came on a grubby beer and wine shop where Ian and I sampled Arak, the local spirit. We were unimpressed and thought it akin to paraffin. Alcohol was expensive and not really worth the effort. Campbell and Alasdair wisely refused to partake, while Roger and Hillbill searched elsewhere. We reunited at 10.00 and piled on to a very busy bus back to the hotel. Donald had driven off with the others and covered some 15 miles around the city and then resorted to walking, without finding any restaurant to their taste. So we had done better! George did without eating altogether. Mosul proved superior to the areas in Baghdad which we encountered. Its eating places were better and regularly supplied knives without being asked. Normally only spoon and fork were supplied, though our seedy restaurant produced carving knives on request.

IRAN (Stages 5, 6 & 7 [part route]) Route

Caspian Sea

□ TEHRAN
Saveh

Kermanshah
Khorramabad
Shahabad
Arak
Malavi
Andimeshk
Susa
Delijan

IRAQ

Isfahan

N
X Pasargadae
X Persepolis
Shiraz

AFGHANISTAN

PAKISTAN

SAUDI
ARABIA

Persian Gulf

Str. of Hormuz

Gulf of Oman

KEY
Scale
0   120 mls
N
X = Naqsh-i-Rajab
-Rustam

Stage 5

Wednesday 18 July - Saturday 21 July

Babylon and the Euphrates; out of Iraq and into Iran; Susa and the Persians

Up after 7.00, with only one rush for the toilet in the night. An improving picture, I think! Showers were our first call and then breakfast. We were offered water eggs – i.e. boiled – or eggs in oil – i.e. fried – served with bread, our own marmalade and a large cup of that ubiquitous tea which is such a delight here. Douglas and I then headed for the local bank, which directed us on again to the main bank, reached through the thronging market area. This was a huge place and we made our way around four great halls as we conducted our business. Returning to the hotel, we filled all our cans with water and prepared for Babylon. The road was well surfaced and we looked forward to seeing the Euphrates at last. So far the Tigris has been our river. It is said that Cyrus the Great, founder of Persia's Achaemenian dynasty captured Babylon by diverting the Euphrates and using the empty river bed to enter the city. There were a lot of trees lining the road for a change and we reached Babylon at the back of 11.00. Our first port of call was the museum so that we could orientate ourselves. This was quite small and disappointing, with most of the originals already seen at the Iraq museum. However, there were several helpful reconstructions to

Restored Ishtar Gate at Babylon

examine. Donald accompanied us on this visit, as he had done also at Aqar Quf. He probably enjoyed the break from driving though he seemed to find the heat very wearing.

We feared that Babylon, for all its great history, being the place chosen as his Eastern capital by Alexander the Great and later to be where Alexander died in 323 BC at the age of 32, might disappoint us. Indeed only the reconstructed works made much sense, notably the Ishtar Gate, the E-Mah temple and the foundations of the palace. Otherwise, the mud brick mounds were confusing and impressed only by their expansive use over the site. We decided against fighting our way a mile out North to see the Babil Mound, site of Nebuchadnezzar's summer palace, though the route would probably have offered the best view of the Euphrates. Instead, we followed the Processional Way, with its paving coated with bitumen to preserve it. This took us to the reconstructed Ishtar gate, mercifully much restored. This monumental Double Gate was massive, built with baked bricks and faced with glazed bricks displaying numerous sacred animals, including the Bull of Hadad and Marduk's serpent headed dragon. We then got access into the restored temple of the goddess Nin-Mah, with brick altar, courtyard and well. Bats twittered around us as we passed along its walls. From here we viewed the Lion of Babylon, a basalt block thought to be a Hittite trophy. Last in the sequence came the restored foundations of the Great Palace of Nebuchadnezzar II where the Hanging Gardens, a wonder of the ancient world, were said to have been located. At this point, Ian and I chose to visit the flattened remains of the mighty ziggurat, E-Temenanki or supposedly the tower of Babel, accompanied by Arab youths. We rejected their customary offers of antiquities and requests for bakshish, glanced

Ishtar Gate: one of Babylon's nine Gates

Lion of Babylon, possibly a Hittite trophy

at the piers of the old bridge made of clay bricks and rejoined the group.

Leaving the site and pausing only for a hamburger and fresh orange juice, we left at 3.30 for Ctesiphon, noted for a sizeable chunk remaining from a Sasanid palace. The impressive arch which survives is in fact part of the great vault or iwan in the south wing. The remaining ruins have vanished. Three German lads were also roaming around the site. We had seen them at Babylon and in the Iraq museum. Another Swiss couple completed the visitor list. At the site we saw over a Bedouin tent and a hut of canes and had a good view too of the Tigris. Back we went to Baghdad where we bought postcards for home and posted them off in a very British looking red post box. Dinner was a curious stew concoction, followed by a meat-filled pancake served with HP sauce. It was certainly different and not considered one of our culinary hits on the trip! We slipped out the hotel and tracked down a wine shop in which we got some white wine before closing time at 9.00. Thus armed, we crept past the boss at our hotel with a tub of ice to make our drink more palatable. It turned out to be sweet and not at all thirst quenching. Roger and George came away from the wine shop with a red wine filled with sediment and rather too sweet for comfort. Despite these slight disappointments, we voted the day a success.

Thursday saw us leaving Baghdad and bound for Iran. We were up by 7.00, breakfasted quickly, paid outstanding bills and said our farewells. We had enjoyed our stay. We drove through Amin Square where we noticed a fine, new statue of Uganda's Idi Amin. He must be favoured by the military! En route, we took note of the large numbers of Ford vehicles and Ford dealers, wondering

Ctesiphon: South wing and vault of Sasanid palace

why there had been all that fuss in Britain over importing our bus. Ford Transit taxis were commonplace. The road to Khanaqin and the frontier seemed devious and progress was slow. Two hours had passed after setting out and we reckoned we were only about a third of the way to our destination. We actually got to Khanaqin soon after 12.00 and found the army again much in evidence as we drew near the frontier, but the road surface was pretty good this time. We used up our Iraqi currency on soft drinks. We also filled our water cans, as the lads had sawn up ice blocks while we were buying cards at the Post Office in Baghdad yesterday and the facility was available there. Never miss a trick!

At the frontier, we first dealt with passports and then on to customs. The place was in confusion, with a guddle of Arabs swarming about and vehicle drivers clustering around for attention. As a result, we were dealt with expeditiously. No vehicle check took place beyond seeing our carnet and we were back on the road within forty minutes, even allowing for a quick orange juice or tea at the frontier. It was, as ever, extremely hot. We passed a quarantine post and then found the gates into Iran closed. Once admitted, we were told unceremoniously that the boss was taking his lunch. We had no choice but to wait for his reappearance and spent a good forty minutes entertained by Arabs having to empty their vehicles totally for customs checks. Once the great man returned from lunch there was much stalling, but at last we secured an amicable outcome, after a total delay of an hour and a half. Off we went into Iran, with our final destination in our sights at last. The country presented a great contrast. Mountains, trees and grassy slopes were all around and the road was excellent.

Our first stop was at Kermanshah, 5,350 feet up, on a large plain between mountains and populated largely by Kurds. Our immediate need was a bank for currency but after a mad search, these were found to be shut. There followed difficult exchanges with feckless police, who seemed determined to avoid appearing decisive, before we were directed by a helpful local through the bazaar to a money exchange office. This met our requirements, though the commission charged was probably high. The National Tourist office was also closed.

Darkness was descending fast as we left for Taq-i-Bustan. There we hoped to find a campsite, according to illuminated adverts seen on the road. We found nothing of the kind. There was however a grassy park, adjacent to the important Sasanid grottoes with bas reliefs and carvings depicting the investiture of the king and hunt scenes. Naturally, our appearance caused a stir, as the park was still crowded and lively.

With help from an Iranian, we got over the language complications and persuaded the site custodian to allow us to camp on the grass. A restaurant was also available and in we marched to feast on hamburger and coke. Cups of tea completed the banquet. We returned to our camp but, finding the park still busy and noisy, a few of us drifted off for a drink to celebrate our arrival in ancient Persia and also to make use of the toilet before the restaurant shut its doors at midnight. So all ended well after all, or so it seemed until the whine of mosquitoes was heard in the tent. These had rarely bothered us on the trip so far and their arrival set us into a state of alarm. In no time we were swathed in towels and perspiring furiously. This did not bode well for the night ahead.

We were up at 6.00, thanks to the early attentions of the custodian who was terrified that we would be found sleeping without a

Susa: work on site below the French protective castle

Susa: column bases and bull headed capitals amid the ruins of Darius' Apadana

permit from the Tourist organisation. The grottoes were still closed and we did not want to spend time there awaiting their opening. We could get a sort of view through the fence and this had to suffice. Coffee followed and then we left for Susa. Lack of any signposts caused us to miss a turn off, a little short of Shahabad, and we had to retrace our course to rejoin the highway south. We now followed 170 kilometres of good road through folded mountains with their outer faces greatly eroded. At Malavi junction, we stopped at a garage and availed ourselves of their water cooler. We also bought some cakes. As we proceeded down the gorge heading for Andimeshk, we passed structured mountain terrain in the foothills of the Zagros mountains, with massive slabs, for all the world like cement, lying in great layers and overlapping at gorges. Roger, our geologist, was in his element!

At Andimeshk, we made enquiries about the Shiraz road. The news was discouraging and we decided to take a detour on our course to Susa, stopping overnight at Andimeshk if the fates favoured. Our original plan to see the massive Elamite ziggurat of Choga Zanbil, the biggest in Iran, had to be abandoned owing to the roads. Ian was unenthusiastic about the detour for Susa. The mountain road failed to impress and he would have preferred a direct course for Persepolis. Still, we made good headway and reached Susa at 2.30. There we waited for the small museum to open at 4.00. A friendly Iranian with his family opened his ice box for our enjoyment while we waited, as our own water was worse than tepid and scarcely drinkable. The temperature today in the vehicle hit 105F.

Susa was where Alexander the Great celebrated a mass wedding ceremony for his 10,000 soldiers with Persian women. Susa had been seat of power first for the Elamites as early as 13th century BC, but later the Assyrians and then Cyrus of Persia seized control and made it his centre. The remains were a bit sparse, though work on the Apadana or audience hall of the palace was in hand. This will make a real difference as the Apadana currently is completely flattened. Yet its fallen remains, and particularly the bull headed capitals, did make an impression. The ancient settlement mound, dating to the 4th millennium, had been cut through and studied. On the acropolis stood the 19th century French castle to protect the Archaeological mission against marauders. Apparently, it has proved its worth over the years! Numerous finds were made on the site and these were to be seen in Tehran and the Louvre. Use of mud bricks caused the impact of the ruins to be greatly lessened, as with Babylon and other sites we have visited. On concluding our visit, we drove back to Andimeshk to hunt for accommodation.

Our first attempt met with refusal by a strict Muslim, who was not much impressed by our shorts and general state. But at this point appeared an RAF officer who put things to right. We ended up on the roof of a small hotel in the town centre with a promise "no mosquitoes" to allay our qualms. The previous night's experience had sharpened our senses and increased our alarm. The price was set under 30 pence. Most of us did clothes washes while waiting for showers. Then out we went with our meagre kitty in quest of sustenance - access to a bank was becoming critical. A restaurant had been recommended to us by the airman and there again an English speaker came across on seeing our confusion over what was on offer. We were moved to a massive table in a spacious side room and were soon tucking into a green salad, a mixed salad of peppers, onions, cucumber and tomato in a tasty sauce, rice and goulash of lentils and meat accompanied by large pitta slices. All this served with jugs of cooled water. It was one of our finest meals to date and cost all of twenty five pence! Hillman cars were far the most common here and Hunters the preferred model. Rootes Motors were clearly flourishing! At this point Hillbill, Ian and I went off to find beer or wine. The station buffet came up trumps, with air conditioning as an extra treat. Our hotel was raging hot inside but a good breeze was blowing on the roof. Mosquitoes were absent and replaced by crowds of cockroaches.

Saturday brought my birthday and departure for Isfahan. We showered, loaded the bus after the ritual coffee and paid our bill. The boss at first asked additional payment for showers but abandoned this when we proved reluctant! We had no success at the local bank and were directed to nearby Dizful, a town so hot in summer that it seems the inhabitants resort to arcaded streets for some shelter! Here two banks refused us, but the central Melli bank did the needful. George had some extra bother with his Scottish cheques but, after heated debate, we were all successful and solvent with local rials. Actually, the bank was very efficient. Only Hillbill and I had brought any Iranian currency from home and so the need for local currency was pressing. We drove across a bridge in the town, only to find at the far side that there was a height restriction, so that Donald had to reverse all the way back - and it was a good distance. Next, we encountered a dead end street - if there was a sign, we did not see it or understand it! As we left the town, we overtook another bus at a toll booth on a bridge and thus swept past without having to pay. There was no pursuit!

Our next stop was Khorramabad which was reached after retracing yesterday's route back to Malavi, before turning off on to new ground. En route, we passed a Sasanid bridge over the river Saimarreh which I was able to photograph. Usually photos were hard to get without significant delay. This eight arched bridge, Pol-i-Doghtar, Daughter's Bridge, dated to Shapur I. It is worth observing here that Iran is peppered with significant archaeological sites and it was as well that we had a firm plan in mind. We had a time scale too! Khorramabad offered an attractively located citadel atop a spur but time again forbade a diversion, though we did make time for a lunch stop with ice cream and cakes. The younger group bought a large melon for the journey. Ian and I then broke away for beer and found Donald and Billco had beaten us to it. Star beer was cheap but not up to the previous Pilsen standard we had found at Andimeshk. When we left for Isfahan, it was obvious we would not be there for nightfall. Still, dealing with the exceptionally juicy melon diverted us as we made for Arak -

not the drink this time but a sizeable town of that name. We decided not to take the shorter route for Isfahan, as that route had stretches of unsurfaced road, according to our information. Our chosen route proved high and scenic.

Arak is comparatively modern and as a result does not figure in the itinerary of the archaeologists. Its main fame lies in carpets. We arrived under cloudy skies at 6.00 and decided to make this our overnight stop. A full tank here cost around £2 and the sight of a garage was welcome, as the tank was low. There followed the normal hotel search. Our first port of call was seedy and seemed pricy for a space on the roof. Instead, while at a bank, we made enquiries and the manager promptly phoned and found us the Arya hotel. Roger had already come upon this and the price quoted was about £1.20 per person. However, the price for the group was dropped to nearer 85 pence and for this we settled. Roger had come up with a cheaper alternative still, but only if we tipped the park watchman and used the public toilet facilities. Being born Sybarites, we stuck with the hotel option! And it was my birthday, after all.

After a good wash, we took a couple of taxis to the centre, though Donald and Bill stayed at the hotel. I am sure the driving must make heavy demands on them. We had been directed to try the Laclac restaurant and the advice was good. We feasted well beside a pool on chicken stuffed omelettes. Ian and I then sampled the national dish, chelo kebab - long grain rice with meat and a slab of butter. This was splendid. Also supplied was mast, a blend of yoghurt and cucumber, plus the usual greens. Soup was evidently a lunch time dish. Wine was pricy and we stuck to beer. On returning to the hotel, my birthday was not forgotten. George produced a half bottle of Arak. This seemed appropriate in view of our staying at Arak! Douglas then dug out a half bottle of whisky - how he had kept this secret so long was nothing short of a marvel - while Roger had a supply of German beer. So we celebrated in some style. The party was over near 1 am.

English is the second language in Iran but rarely understood. Yet they certainly outdo us in the range of languages being used! A common facial feature seemed to be a rather fleshy nose and deep-set beady eyes, from our observation since entering the country. No showers were available in the hotel.

IRAN (Stages 5, 6 & 7 [part route]) Route -·-·-

Caspian Sea

TEHRAN
Saveh

Kermanshah
Khorramabad
Shahabad
Arak
Delijan
IRAQ
Malavi
Andimeshk
Susa

Isfahan

N
X
X   X Pasargadae
Persepolis
Shiraz

AFGHANISTAN

P
A
K
I
S
T
A
N

SAUDI
ARABIA

Persian Gulf

Str. of Hormuz

Gulf of Oman

KEY
Scale
0   120mls

N
X = Naqsh-i-Rajab
      -Rustam

113

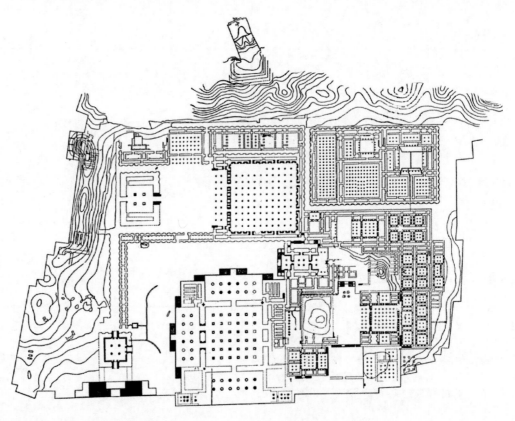

Main Apadana with stairways (centre foot)
Small Central Palace with North stairway (above and immediately right of Apadana)
Hall of 100 Columns (above and half right). Treasury of Darius (top right).

Stage 6

Sunday 22 July - Tuesday 24 July

Isfahan; Pasargadae; Persepolis

We slept well, though Campbell and George were suffering a little from our party of the previous night. A select few of us were in an attractive room looking on to a yard, while most were on the floor below. We kept the fan going all night and this made for greater comfort. The hotel gave us three fried eggs each, on fresh bread served with tea. After a quick but necessary clean of the interior of the bus, we set off at 9.00 for Isfahan, said to be "an oasis in the desert". We had a stop at Delijan for a refreshing glass of mast. This Iranian delight consists of yoghurt with mint and cucumber, sometimes served as a drink and as a side dish at other times. It is most refreshing, whatever its consistency. The price was cheekily high considering the awful ramshackle premises in which we were served, but they were bold enough even to add insult to injury and seek alms. They must have thought we looked prosperous! The reality is, of course, that tourists are always assumed to be wealthy, regardless of their background. Cloud and even the odd shower accompanied us as we made for Isfahan, where we arrived before 4.00 and found a place to park by the river. We intended to sightsee and what a city it proved!

Far and away the most beautiful of all the places we have visited, Isfahan owes much of its splendour and magnificent mosques and

A view of Isfahan's splendour

Bridge of 33 Arches into Isfahan, dating to Shah Abbas in 16/17th centuries

palaces to Shah Abbas the Great, who made the city his capital in 1598. Our time frame of two hours permitted us merely to scratch the surface but we were all greatly impressed. We paid for entry to some of the buildings, getting student rates, and Campbell, Ian and I attempted a mini tour of the principal area. We finished up at the great bazaar, leading out of the striking Royal Square. During our walk, a passing motor cyclist made a snatch at Campbell's camera. He held on grimly and the cyclist gave up the attempt. There were carpets on sale everywhere. They numbered thousands, often a bit drab and purposely looking old. Many were laid out for passers-by to cross them, as this was a sign of their quality.

Hotel prices decreed that we should make for the Youth hostel, despite some opposition from Donald, who would have preferred to find the campsite. The hostel was new and cost us a bit over 60 pence, or less if you were a hostel member. We were not long in getting settled. A young chap from Tabriz was staying at the hostel and he packed us into his jeep and dropped us at a restaurant where we started with a lovely soup along with a half chicken. The owner was amazed when we went on to ask for rice, spinach and a meat sauce. Of course, he was unaware how meagre our diet often was. Tea concluded the feast. Being strictly Muslim premises, no alcohol was served. Women also were eating in the restaurant and we saw them in the mosques as well. This was unusual up till now, hence worthy of comment. They wore sombre shawls in variegated colours rather than black as seen in most countries till now. The meal was a bargain at 60 pence or so. On returning to our hostel, we found them selling beer in pints and they presented us with a lively spectacle and noisy singsong. They kept serving till midnight, though we had been told that everything would stop at 11.00. As you might expect, we were not complaining!

Monday was to be an early start into the world of ancient Persia at last. Most of the party surfaced around 6 am. Showers were appreciated though cold. We were all charged the rate for hostel members, though only half of us were true blue. Breakfast was made up of scones with cheese and butter plus carrot and cherry jams. Coffee and tea were also offered. As one coffee after another was taken, it became clear that the early start was drowning in caffeine. Donald needed his morning hit. We eventually left at 8.00 and spent the early part of the journey playing solo. Passing the university, we set off along desert-like country bounded by distant mountains on either side. Greenock George was still suffering stomach disorder and the sight of miles of scrubland and no trees alarmed him. He cheered up no end when occasional trees began to reappear. His luck got better still when we arrived at a military post and he was allowed to use the toilet there. Our next brief call was at a teashop where George sailed into seven eggs. I was not convinced that this was the best treatment for a dodgy stomach but let it pass. The road now began to climb steadily and reached a height upwards of 7,000 feet. Scrub continued to surround us. We were now entering the province of Fars, heart of ancient Persia, where the countryside was awash with ancient remains. The condition of roads had deteriorated greatly and steep descents with hairpin bends were standard.

A turn off the main road led us to Pasargadae, which Cyrus of Persia had made his capital around 546 BC. His tomb remains there and was visited by Alexander, a huge fan of Cyrus the Great. Royalty visited the site in 1971 and greatly simplified directions for

Size matters: Roger measures up to a tall pillar with resident storks in the Apadana at Pasargadae

Tomb of Cyrus the Great at Pasargadae

later tourists like ourselves. First, on paying entry as students, we went to the tomb itself, made of massive stones and standing high on a plinth. We were instructed by a custodian not to consider climbing up to see inside. Anyway, it was empty! Next, we passed the remains of the Residential Palace followed by the Audience Hall where a single column survived of the original eight and this the residence of three storks and a single nest. Bases of the columns and doorways were of black limestone and striking. Otherwise, limestone was the norm in the palace area - a welcome change from friable mud bricks. Bas reliefs and inscriptions in various languages could be seen. Moving Northwards, we saw the Palace of Gates, most ruined of them all, but with a unique four-winged figure on one door jamb. We continued to a square tower on a plinth, seemingly a religious building, and finally to a great stone platform fitted with metal clamps. Most of the remains were hard to understand and mud brick construction in some outer buildings made things even harder. Provision for helicopters to land could be seen near Cyrus' tomb and traces of red carpeting were visible on stone floors. Again, a throw back to recent royal visits.

Clouds came over as the afternoon advanced. We encountered a few tourist buses at the site as well as three tourist cars. This was a change! Usually, we were pretty much on our own when going around the sites. We passed Persepolis as we made for Shiraz. It was dim under cloudy skies at the foot of a mountain and was approached by a poplar lined avenue. A great, illuminated yellow sign pointed the way. A bank too was provided. That would be for us next day!

A wrong turn when we reached Shiraz cost us a little time and irritation till we secured clear directions to the campsite. There, Donald was all for saving some pence and pitching our own tents on a gravel surface. He was outvoted and we chose rather the site's own tents at 60 pence per tent. These were airy and spacious, with room for three in a tent. There was a swimming pool and we snatched this luxury before taking showers. Then we piled into an open backed van from the campsite into town. We had been directed to the Honey restaurant where we started with a rather dilute tomato soup as precursor to a tasty shrimp salad. After a couple of beers locally, we headed back to the tents for 11.00.

The differential on the bus was markedly noisier today and we enquired about garages. Apparently, our only hope was either Tehran or Istanbul. I suppose that should have been obvious but we had hoped for better. There was a minitrek at the site which hailed from Bristol and they were travelling on a minibus identical to ours. The main difference was that they were flown out to Istanbul to start their trek. There were 14 of them plus driver. Evidently, they were allowed just an hour to see Persepolis. We had definitely grander expectations! We heard from various sources that we did well to avoid the mountain road between Shiraz and Susa, as it was truly atrocious.

We were up by 7.00 for a morning swim at the campsite and then showers, followed by a substantial breakfast. This was the great day and the fulfilment of the purpose of the project. We made use of the bank seen the previous night outside Persepolis and made good use too of their chilled water. The longer the tellers took, the more water we drank! We guessed that we would soon feel the need for this. At the entry, we paid little more than 10 pence as members of a student group. We set out into the site at 10.30 and I was last to emerge at 2.30, with shoulders burned,

Persepolis: Xerxes Gate with its double portal

Opposite: Looking over the Hall of 100 Columns to Darius' Apadana to right and showing Darius' Palace and Xerxes' Palace to left of the Apadana. The modern reception area lies outside beyond the site buildings

North stair into Central Palace showing Median nobles and courtiers in bas relief

Crack Persian troops on East stair of Apadana at Persepolis

Symbol of Ahura Mazda in the Central Palace

Xerxes fights a mythical monster in the Hall of 100 columns

Homage is paid to Darius by a Median official

Vassals bring their offerings to the Great King

Stairs lead from the Apadana to the Central Palace

*Rock cut tomb of Artaxerxes II above the site: king worshipping at
a fire altar below Ahura Mazda symbol*

Naqsh-i-Rostem: tombs of Darius (extreme left), Xerxes and (in the sun, facing) Artaxerxes I or Darius II

Naqsh-i-Rostem: tomb of Artaxerxes I (or Darius II) with a Sasanid joust carved below

soaked with perspiration and dehydrated - but thoroughly satisfied. I was limping too as a result of a nail going right through the sole of my sandal during walkabout.

What then of the site? Spectacular would not do it justice. Following the plan, we tried to see everything of significance and take photographs, with our classical studies course back home in mind. I set the camera at 500th of a second to allow for shake in my hands caused by exertion under a blazing sun. First, we viewed the column capitals, as we wanted to take advantage, as far as possible, of the position of the sun. Lions, bulls and a number of other creatures were represented. Xerxes' Gateway of all the Nations got us going. The sun also determined my rush to get to a high point beside the rock cut tombs of Artaxerxes II and III, from where — with the sun behind — a good view was to be had over the site, not to mention the rows of tents beyond the site, a small town in themselves. These were presumably to house the parties of dignitaries visiting the site.

On we went to the splendid Apadana or Reception Hall of Darius and Xerxes and the North Palace to view the staircases with the amazing bas reliefs showing the Immortals, crack Persian troops and the king's bodyguard, Persian nobles chatting together and foreign dignitaries bringing gifts and leading livestock to honour the great king. Images of the great god Ahura Mazda were also frequently shown. Again, the position of the sun was vital for all these photographs! These figures were like a photographic record of what actually happened in the great reception hall and would have been brightly painted, as with much of the magnificent buildings all around. This was unforgettable and I prayed my camera would do justice to the spectacle. On returning home to Britain, I found the only problem was occasional over exposure caused by the brilliance of the light. I am not expert enough to know how to counter this!

When we reached the museum at noon, we found it closed till 2.00, so back we went to see the palaces of Darius and Xerxes, the Halls of 32 columns, 100 columns and 99 columns, as well as the earlier mentioned rock cut tombs. The massive three level terrace and the complex drainage bore witness to the meticulous planning which had preceded the building on the site. Though never the capital, nor the administrative capital like Susa, Persepolis was the residence favoured by Darius and his successors. Building began under Darius from around 520 BC. When Alexander arrived in 330 BC and burned the palace, it was thought he did this to avenge the hurt done to the Greeks by the Persian invaders. Views differ and drink could have played a part - it does seem a bit out of character for Alexander. Quite apart from the stairways with their fabulous bas reliefs, numerous bull figures and animals were dotted around the site, to say nothing of the many inscriptions. Fine bas reliefs in the Treasury depicted Darius enthroned with nobles and attendants, while Xerxes had his moment in the Hall of 100 columns in contest with fabulous monsters! If this was how he pictured himself in advance of his invasion of Greece, he certainly was in for a disappointment. Other buildings made of mud brick presumably housed soldiers and domestics. Finally, we got to the museum, rather an anticlimax and disappointing after the splendour outside. We concluded the visit by returning to the tomb of Artaxerxes for our final view. When we returned to the bus, we found Donald poring over the map. We purchased cards and stamps on site while Billco completed oil change and greasing in readiness for the return journey.

Heading back for Shiraz, we paused briefly at Naqsh-i-Rajab to see the three rock carved tombs of Sasanid kings mounted on chargers.

Still not content, we stopped again at Naqsh-i-Rustam. Here we were back with the Persian Achaemenian dynasty and the rock cut tombs of Darius and three of his successors. Achaemenian fire altars were also there to be studied. We had a battle to secure student rates for the party but ended successfully. Darius II alone was in sunshine, while Darius, Xerxes and Artaxerxes I were in shade. Carvings depicted the kings in the presence of the winged symbol of Ahura Mazda. Interestingly, Sasanid rulers had carved their own reliefs next to and below the Achaemenian ones. Fire temples and altars were also to be seen at the site. It being 4.00, the clouds rolled in and there was a sharp shower as we made for Shiraz. Perfect timing again!

I realised, once I had time to recover, that I was a bit scorched, in common with most of the others, and my foot was throbbing. Clearly, I needed to see Hillbill for dressings from the medical kit. Donald had noted the temperature in the sun and found it running at 138 F. He also reckoned that we had now driven 6,700 miles. Bill and he have done brilliantly at the wheel and the bus too has been a wonder, considering the climbs and roads that it has faced. When we returned to the campsite in Shiraz, water could not be drunk between the hours of 6 and 10 in the evening and that was a useful opportunity to give the bus a thorough wash. After a swim and shower and with a dressing on my foot, we again took a taxi into the centre for a meal. There we split up and I did well for myself at a pizzeria. Perhaps not very Persian, but not Italian either, as I indulged in a tasty schnitzel. The shop was out of beer when we returned to the camp, but Donald had thoughtfully laid aside a few for emergencies like this! None of us felt up to a late night and we retired early, just as the hosing of the lawns began. We hoped this would not rouse any mosquitoes to action in the night.

While the group was traversing the site, Billco had greased the propeller shafts and cleaned the bolts. The differential remained noisy but we remained optimistic and imagined that we would find a decent garage in Tehran or, failing that, in Istanbul. Our original scheme to divert and visit the Black Sea and the Caspian on the homeward seemed less likely now, owing to reports of bad roads and high mountain passes.

Stage 7

Wednesday 25 July - Sunday 29 July

***The homeward trek begins; Isfahan, Tehran
and Tabriz; and back into Turkey***

After our early night, we were up for an early
start on Wednesday, soon after 6.00. Showers
preceded coffee and we noted we were now
on our last two gas containers. Bill admitted
that, after his efforts on the engine, he had
fallen asleep for the best part of an hour in the
toilet! My breakfast was a mighty tub of fresh
yoghurt. Departure was slightly delayed by
some of the group seizing a moment for a last
swim and then the homeward trek began. I
resorted to different sandals, as they appeared
to provide better padding and support for my
sore foot. We had a brief tea stop at Surmaq
and called at another further along at Khaneh
Khereh for Campbell to retrieve a mug which
he had inadvertently left on our outward run.
Our route again took us past Persepolis and
the royal tombs. Happy memories!

Several villages in the area were fortified
by mud walling. It was quite thin and
occasionally round towers had been added.
We also saw a number of working brick kilns
along our route. These were piled inside
great conical towers of fancily shaped bricks,
then smothered with mud casings in which
vents were supplied and finally left to bake.
Pigeon towers were another feature and a
very occasional camel. Farms appeared at

The dreaded sleeping sickness claims two victims

We pause briefly at primitive Margan village

Always on the search for photos with my old Zenith camera

Ian and I assess local interest and curiosity

regular intervals and we marvelled at the old winnowing technique in action - throwing up grain and chaff into the air and letting the wind separate out the grain. Large areas, almost like national parks, bore signs indicating that no shooting or hunting was allowed. Back in the cities, we noticed that the Iranians were dreadful jaywalkers - they would feel at home in Glasgow! They were careless to the point of suicidal and quite oblivious to vehicles starting off. Horns made no impression and no doubt the fault would rest with the driver in the event of an accident.

Several heavy showers accompanied our journey back to Isfahan. It was pelting and water came in at Donald's door as well as at the passenger door. We wondered if this was caused by settling. We returned to the Youth hostel on reaching Isfahan around 5.00 and found it much busier than previously. In fact, they had to put in extra beds to accommodate us. Showers freshened us all up before we headed into town. I took another glance around the bazaar, but again nothing of interest caught my eye. George, however, was more determined and bought an Afghan coat for about £15. It seemed a fine purchase and he was mightily pleased. We feasted well near the Turkish Baths, stopped off for a few beers and then nine of us forced ourselves into a Fiat taxi to return to the hostel. Again, we had an early night after a nightcap on the verandah.

Roger's account reports that he tied up my pyjama legs today but I make no reference to this in my diary. I suppose my many school trips had accustomed me to such escapades and this was a fairly tame assault as these things go. So I took it in my stride, once the knots were undone!

Another day nearer home and we were up and about by 6 am. Donald was desperate for a leisurely breakfast ahead of the expected turmoil of Tehran. So we had leisure to look around and noticed another minitrek group had appeared in the night and must also have found space at the hostel. We took coffees at the hostel café and the cost differed greatly from the night before. Addition was clearly not their forte. We let it stand, even though the price was increased, as we were eager to hit the road. This we managed by 8.00. We took several wrong turnings around Tehran and saw unfamiliar parts. Donald always hated asking for guidance and preferred to drive till something familiar or a signpost appeared. This did not work well for us on this occasion! We had a brief tea stop at noon and another was forced on us when the engine began overheating as we embarked on a steady, prolonged climb. We had been forced to accept lower grade petrol at a garage which had no super grade on offer and no doubt this was the consequence. The day seemed exceptionally hot and we were glad to get back into the shelter of the bus once things returned to normal.

About 10 kilometres out of Tehran, we stopped at a campsite at Saveh, a small, attractive town. There we unloaded our kit while Donald and Bill tried to phone the Ford garage in Tehran. This failed and they decided to drive into town. This too ended in failure. Meanwhile, we put up the tents and off loaded our baggage into them, before having a wash. Next, seven of us took a taxi into Tehran, as currency was failing again. There was the usual haggle over the price but we reckoned we came out best. Banks were, as usual, closed as it was approaching evening and we went to exchange shops. We had not yet abandoned hope of seeing the Caspian Sea! That aspiration took us to the British Embassy, as we found the Iranians a bit aloof and unwilling or unable to offer advice. We wanted help with possible bus trips. The Embassy was massive, heavily guarded and fenced, and with resplendent double gates flanked by a huge lion and unicorn on either side. Our timing was lucky and we found a young lad who proved very helpful, once he had recovered from the shock of finding us at the door. He told us that the tour bus would take four hours to make the trip there. Food for thought!

So off we went for sustenance and a pint of draught beer en route. At the restaurant, chicken and lemon soup was on offer, followed by meat and rice with a bean stew. This was very acceptable. As we left to get a taxi, Hillbill threw up on the street, blaming it on the poor roads and heat during the day. What with his recurring nose bleeds, he was suffering more than the rest of us at this point in the trip. Our taxi was a big Mercedes and the driver regaled us with English records as we made for the central square and a bus to the campsite. Things got better still when Ian found a friendly farmer who loaded us on to the back of his truck - it had metal seats and an open top. He charged us not a rial for the open top tour! Donald and Bill were back waiting at the camp. The garage had been closed and so our last hope was Istanbul. We would try to make an early start. Those of us who used the camp grounds found them hard, dusty and alive with ants. Ian and Hillbill wisely chose to take beds in the dormitories. The swimming pool was being cleaned and so we were denied this pleasure. Roger asked for eggs at the camp buffet, where they were listed among beverages. They came raw with tops removed! There was no sign of any hot water if we were meant to boil them. Life is full of surprises.

Ian heard that there had been a coup in Afghanistan and 3,000 people were stuck at the frontier. We wondered how this would have affected us if we had been passing through Iraq at this juncture, with our visas stamped Royal Afghan Embassy, now that the monarchy had been overthrown by the military. Our foreign trips have previously met with military movements which could have proved troublesome. Our earliest expedition took us to Tunisia in 1967 at the time of the Six Day War, with Israel fighting Egypt, Jordan and Syria. Then in 1969, when we travelled along the North African coast from Algeria to Libya, we narrowly missed being interned, thanks to Gaddafi's uprising against King Idris. But this expedition to Persepolis in 1973 took the biscuit, what with an attempted coup in Iraq as we headed towards our destination and next a military coup close by in Afghanistan. The ancient gods kept us in their sights!

Friday morning saw us up at 5 am. I slept quite well, apart from one awakening by a diesel engine somewhere in the night. The rail track passed near the camp. It was cool almost too cold in the night and I felt it, having foregone my pyjama jacket - my usual state in the hotter nights hitherto. I enjoyed a really hot shower and a cold freshener before taking morning coffee. We were out of Tehran by 6.45 and on to a real freeway with toll payable. This marvel took us for a pittance on the road to Karaj, a small town popular with the people of Tehran for its small river setting. As ever, the double deck buses held our attention: AECs, Guys and a few Albions. There were also some angular looking, more modern Leylands painted green and we wondered if this heralded a colour change for the city. Campbell left some small change in the shower, but it had gone when he went to retrieve it. We paid a little over £2 in Iran for a full tank though poorer quality petrol came at about half that. We preferred to keep to higher octane to boost performance.

The motorway presented a new challenge for us, with cars coming up the slipway facing oncoming traffic. This appeared to be a ruse for dodging tolls, as these were paid on entry and not when leaving the motorway. Tehran had two types of taxi and both expensive to our thinking. Orange ones were metered, whereas blue ones were slightly cheaper and unmetered. As we made for Qasvin, an important wine centre and note the 'vin' in its name, we were invaded by a mighty hornet, which caused an immediate panic and forced us to stop at the roadside for emergency evacuation. The beast proved amenable and left quietly. In we piled again and sped over a good road surface until the engine began to overheat and we took a brief refreshment stop. On we pressed and crossed the Qisil Usun and then entered the dark gorge of the river. The rail track ran near the road. Soon we reached Mianeh at 4,850 feet. We passed through two lengthy tunnels on this stretch. Mianeh stood on an important cross roads and was fought over from early times. Here we paused to park at the bus station and enjoy an excellent lunch of messy melons.

We were now in Azerbaijan province with a great population mix. Turks, Russians and others have claimed it over the years and it suffered greatly from the Mongol invasion in the 13th century. It presented a green and mountainous face. Bus drivers were a menace on the highway, delighting in overtaking at high speed on blind corners and forcing smaller vehicles into the gutter. We heard that one bus crashed through a bridge at Gorgan two days back, killing over 40 of its 60 passengers. In hindsight, we were lucky to have escaped the infamous "fast and first" style of driving in Tehran. We escaped that city unscathed. A second hornet shot in the bus window on the Mianeh stretch but this one hit me in the face and dropped between me and my seat. A quick dose of insecticide by Billco resolved this crisis and restored calm. The panic caused when such a hornet entered the van would have to be seen to be believed. The bus would rush to the roadside and everyone would launch themselves out to safety, returning only when the threat passed. Billco's swift application of insecticide on this occasion was therefore most timely and saved the emergency drill! Apart from a few rough sections, the road was good and only its height, rising to over 6,000 feet, caused the bus any discomfort. In consequence, we made better time than expected and we were at the outskirts of Tabriz by 5.30.

Finding the campsite took some time and poor road signs were largely to blame. Here, we hired tents and these were spacious and comfortable. Showers were limited and the site seemed to double as a public park and play area around a lake. Insects and people were about equal in numbers. Turkish influence and language was very marked. Once encamped, we took showers before finding a bus into the centre. This was not entirely straightforward, as we failed the requirement to hold boarding tickets. A sympathetic driver let us on and took us to the nearest kiosk to obtain the needful. Tabriz was large and busy with a large Turkish population. We found a self service restaurant which made paying bills a great deal simpler than was often the case in our travels. Usually, we all fought over the exact amount we had eaten and paid only what we thought was due. It was not always so, but often it could end up like this when ready cash was running low! The meal was substantial and well priced. Soup and mast were popular. Water and orange drink were the accompaniments. We took a taxi back to the campsite, having failed to work out the bus system, despite prolonged study at a bus kiosk. We had a couple of beers at the camp, with police in attendance, before the bar shut at 11.00. The barman tried to get us to pay service but we pointed out that we had served ourselves and the police seemed happy with this and supported us! The people in the camp area had the decency to begin dispersing around 10.30, not so the insects! There was no water available when we headed off to bed.

The night was cool and we slept well. After all, Tabriz stands at some 4,450 feet up. George indeed wore his newly purchased Afghan coat in bed. It was again verging on cold at one point when I woke in the night to deal with a blood beetle on my leg. It was 6.15 am when we rose and found the insects ready and waiting to feast on us. Donald was less than enthusiastic about getting up this morning, until he got the whiff of coffee brewing. We contented ourselves with cold showers and were eager to make a quick get away - Roger had pulled the toilet cistern off the wall when pulling the chain last night and we did not want this to be noticed! The cistern was embossed " Seamless Liverpool cast iron toilet". A little officious chap in important braid was at the seat of custom. He failed to realise that we had been sleeping in their tents and not our own. So we got a bargain. Tabriz railway station looked new and was very splendid seen from the outside as we departed.

Most of us were hoping to cross into Turkey if we made good time, though Donald declared he would be happy to stop over at Maku, just short of the border. Amazingly, we reached Maku around noon. Route 4 from Tabriz was excellent, with careful gradients. The scenery was fine with mountain valleys, trees and plenty flowers. Only one section was poor when the road passed through a barren, dusty plain, which looked as though it must flood in winter. Here, we met several tour buses bouncing along and throwing clouds of dust over us. New bridges were being constructed at this section and ugly diversions resulted. Thirst forced us to make a brief stop for Pepsi at a tiny village with mud huts, where roofing was hay and dung pancakes seemed to serve for fuel. Maku was the excuse for a longer pause and we marvelled at its precarious position below a cliff face. An ancient rampart wound its way up either side of the cliff face. Shops claiming to sell tourist goods turned out to be general stores. Banks also let us down and referred us to the frontier to change money but one shop with whitewashed windows offered the consolation of beer in its gloomy interior.

On we pressed, viewing with wonder far off Mount Ararat, all 17,000 feet of it and with snow crowning the summit. Such magnificence! Turkey was drawing close and soon we were passing through the Iranian frontier. Our passage here was swift, a mere 20 minutes, in the company of a couple of British Land Rovers, some Italians and two lorries. One of the Italians had all his car papers stolen in Morocco and could show only a letter from the Moroccan police. Next came an even briefer call at the Turkish frontier where only our passports and vehicle carnet were examined. We spent a necessary 20 minutes at the bank to obtain Turkish liras before proceeding for Agri. We were now free from Iran and the indemnity requirement for the bus. Glasgow Corporation could breathe a sigh of relief!

The road was at first deplorable and badly rutted and with potholes. We saw a couple of large eagle-like birds at a wayside stream. We had seen similar birds on Nemrut Dağı and that seemed a long time in the past. About 30 kilometres short of Agri, we stopped for a refreshing tea. The road continued bad and

8,000 feet up near Tahir en route Erzurum

cobbles in the villages added to our general discomfort. It was after 6.00 when we bounced into Agri and went off to hotel hunt. First appearances proved deceptive and we found several possibilities around the bus station. We settled for the Gök hotel at about 25 pence a person, with a small additional charge for much needed showers. Splendid new sandals were laid out in each room - they still had the price labels attached! Agri stands around 5,000 feet up and so the evening was cool. A tributary of the Euphrates passed nearby. The hotel boss sent out his son to lead us to his recommended restaurant and his taste proved good. We celebrated our return to Turkey with a raki before feasting on excellent slabs of fish served with salad and fresh bread. Wine too was freely available. Ian got into an argument with an elderly lady doctor from South Africa in the restaurant and the rest of us left him to it. Donald and Bill stayed at the hotel. The night concluded with a medley of Scottish songs, probably a rare occurrence in these parts!

Sunday morning saw most of the group rather subdued after the night's merriment. We packed and paid and took several cups of tea before heading off on a dust road. Actually, it was fine and level, a big improvement on potholes. The mountain scenery was great and we stopped at 8,000 feet above Tahir for views and watched an army convoy struggling past. The air was cool and the mountain vegetation a delight. On reaching Erzurum, a substantial and important town in the province, we had a lunch stop for 40 minutes and sampled soup and yoghurt with ice cream to finish. The price was negligible. The usual crowd gathered around to spectate while we enjoyed our ices. Before entering Erzurum, the road had become asphalt and well-maintained. This improvement continued all the way to Erzincan.

Our route took us down the Euphrates valley and we crossed various bridges over the river and accompanying railway. We passed through Erzincan at 4.30 and pressed on with Sivas our goal. Nothing deflected us from our plan as Zara, a small town on the route, offered no hotels to interest us.

Darkness was falling by this time and we paused briefly at a tour coach restaurant on the road for döner kebab to tide us over. The road reverted to dust and pebble after Zara but it remained reasonable. We ignored a diversion sign intended to lead us round a small town and this proved wise, as being a lot shorter. None the less, it was after 10.00 when we reached Sivas and began the hotel hunt. Sivas boasted some important monuments but we had no time for these. We chose an indifferent hotel for convenience, as we were all weary and Donald and Billco had been sorely tested by the roads. Its name, Hotel Divan, probably played a part in winning us over. The accommodation was just tolerable but low priced. It also proved rather a squeeze to get us all ensconced and lacked showers. Finding a decent restaurant was also a pain in our weary state but we managed after a search. That doner kebab earlier was a blessing!

Petrol stop near Iran frontier

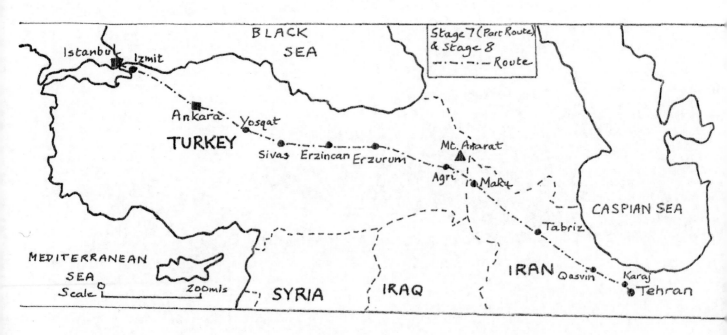

Stage 8

Monday 30 July - Thursday 2 August

Istanbul in focus

We woke at 7.00 and borrowed a brush from the hotel to give the bus a good sweep. This was only the third major clean out of the interior on the trip and the clean up was much overdue! 30 minutes were allocated for breakfast and I managed within the time to buy stamps at a local post office. All that I needed now was post cards! Then it was off on the road to Ankara while most of the company slept. I continued my reading of *War and Peace* which had taken up my time intermittently. At 12.30 we reached Yozgat, a town known to us from last year's trip to Syria and Jordan. There, we had a lunch stop and enjoyed the fresh, cool breeze blowing through the town. Postcards of Yozgat were on sale in the shops to my surprise, as the town seemed to offer little of significance to visitors. The stamps which I had obtained a while earlier now had back-up! Banking gave us the usual problem and we had to wait for George and Roger being led back to us after a conducted tour in the back streets to locate a suitable bank. A little group of fascinated children milled around us as we waited beside the bus. Once again, Roger got his name altered to Koger when making his transaction in the bank. The afternoon was given over to solo, chess and whist to pass time.

At Üsküdar (Scutari), looking to the West. The new bridge nears completion

At 5.00 we were on the outskirts of Ankara and traffic increased and the quality of driving took a downward spiral. Donald coped admirably, but chose to bypass the capital and head out towards Istanbul where we had noted a campsite. This meant a disappointment for the majority, as they had never seen Ankara and its many attractions. We got to the campsite at 6.00 and sat out in the fading sun after a shower. There was no restaurant and we contented ourselves with such food as could be bought in the camp store. Choice was limited but we managed to present a palatable dinner with wine to wash it down. Another group from England joined us and a merry night ensued.

Our rather late night made for a rather later than usual reveille and a lethargic feel to the day. Still, we hit the road by 8.00, eager to get to Istanbul. We stopped for lunch at the Vine mocamp and after that we had our first glimpse of the sea again at Izmit. It seemed an age since our last encounter with the sea at Pamuçak and we could well understand how Xenophon and his Ten Thousand Greeks felt on seeing the sea again after their long march inland. The road surface had some pretty bumpy sections but work on a dual carriageway was in progress. Traffic became increasingly heavy and, as we neared Istanbul, as at Ankara, driving standards plummeted. The air was cool and a brisk breeze freshened us all. The ferry from Üsküdar across the Bosphorus had us over in no time to the west.

Everywhere were the fine old ferries, many Clyde built and a pleasure to the eye. Our modern looking sisters built at Fairfields on the Clyde were much in evidence and still cock of the walk. I was whisked back to thoughts of watching them fitting out from the deck of *Queen Mary II* in the good old days when I was working on the Doon the Watter

The attractive group of Fairfield ferries fitting out in July 1961 for the long trip to Istanbul

run from Bridge Wharf. The new bridge across the strait too was nearing completion and I wondered what impact this might have on the ferry fleet. There was also a fine, two funnel yacht at anchor, together with some destroyers and several cruise ships and merchant vessels. Joy was unconfined! What a city!

We had earlier decided to spend a bit more time here in view of its many attractions, to prepare us for the final push back home. Consultation at the student office resulted in our making for the Tourist hostel beside Aghia Sophia, a very upmarket location. Unfortunately, the hostel was mobbed and offered little attraction in its residents or facilities. The price, however, suited us. We were careful to deposit valuables in the safe before taking hot showers and launching ourselves on the city in quest of food. This entailed quite a search, as none of the places first visited seemed to have the food we wanted ready for eating. Even the fish restaurants around Galata Bridge failed us. So we ended up in a slightly upmarket restaurant where the food was good but the prices far above what had become our norm. We saved on tips, which were refused, despite the pressure from waiters! Back in the streets, we finished our meal with ice cream before adjourning to the hostel for beer. I took a top bunk and hoped for a quiet night. The hostel was still noisy and seemed a bit run down.

Dawn brought us into August and we were up by 8.00, with plans to do some sightseeing. First, I took a very hot shower and a cold one to follow. Next, we headed out for breakfast, picked up our cameras from the office safe and went off to do some shopping in the Grand or Covered Bazaar. I ended up with a selection of leather bags, a tea set consisting of traditional glass cups with metal saucers and

Roman Landward walls at Istanbul

little spoons and some Turkish tea to complete the setting. I had thought of alabaster items but these proved costly. I did, however, invest in an ashtray. Copper goods were too bulky and I considered the kaftans to be drab and unattractive. Jewellery too did not appeal. All of us had a lively time in the Bazaar, entering into the spirit of haggling. Time allotted was 90 minutes, but finding one's way about was tricky and it was no surprise that we were two down when the time came to move on. George and Hillbill failed to show after a reasonable time was allowed and we abandoned them to the Bazaar and headed for the Blue Mosque. This could not fail to impress and was an eye opener for those who were seeing it for the first time. Next came a visit to Topkapi and we left our cameras at the entry rather than pay for taking them with us. We all marvelled at the lavish life styles of the sultans with their diamonds, emeralds and assorted weaponry. The circumcision room was closed to us, though there was a gathering of young victims awaiting the knife. Also on show were hairs from Mahomet's beard and body parts of John the Baptist contained in a bronze arm. As we left the palace, we sniggered, I hoped unobtrusively, at the rolling goose step of the soldiers performing the changing of the guard. From the palace we made for the hostel, sublime to ridiculous, to change into shorts, now that we had seen inside the Blue Mosque.

Having missed us at the Bazaar, George and Bill had lunch in the area. The draw of the Bazaar had proved too much and it was hard to find one's way around. The rest of us made our own lunch arrangements before taking a trolley bus to the Edirne Gate in the city walls. It was here that Mehmet II forced entry into the city in 1453 and caused the city's fall. Nearby was the Church of the Holy Saviour,

Kahriye Camii, dating back to 6th century AD and famed for its remarkable mosaics. This we visited along with others and were distressed by the deterioration of Christian churches in the city. But the condition of the Roman walls was much worse. A mighty chasm had been dug into the walls at the Edirne Gate for a new road and they were attacking the job with gusto, using picks and shovels. We followed the course of the landward wall through dumps, latrines, shanty housing and livestock. Even restored sections seemed to be abused and the Seaward Gate was particularly bad. Modern roads broke the wall line frequently, causing us to make detours. We even encountered a railway. Some of the original lesser gates survived in reasonable repair. It was a long, interesting march and we enjoyed refreshments at its conclusion, before taking a bus back to Sirkeçi and the hostel at 6 pm. There we showered and changed before going out into the town. We found an excellent restaurant where bolder spirits took mackerel while I played safe with meat soup and shish kebab - and yoghurt, of course! Born and brought up at the coast, my mother had always shunned mackerel as a dirty fish and the belief still lingered with me. The service charge was high but the meal was well priced and high quality. Needless to say, no one suffered any harm from the mackerel!

Next day, we agreed to enjoy a further day free from travel to savour the fascination of Istanbul. The weather was cloudy though bright and there was always a threat of rain. The previous day had been similar but less windy. After showers, we breakfasted at the hostel. Yoghurt and omelette were available though service was rather slow. Then we headed for the quayside and boarded a boat for Büyük Ada, the largest of the Princes' Islands in the Sea of Marmara. Following instruction, we took a direct sailing to allow us to complete the return trip in one day. Our ship, *Maltepe*, was diesel and left a little late after 10.30. We reached the terminus within 2 hours. The sun struggled to shine through the cloud and we struggled to find a beach. The best we could get was a concrete platform with a charge for swimming. We decided to keep our cash rather for wine or beer and took a horse and trap back to the pier for the 2.30 sailing. This time our ship was the *Fenerbahçe*, a 1953 Denny product, sporting a picture of her Clyde launch in the saloon. She was again an express and fair rushed us back to the city with a slight detour for a closer look at the US aircraft carrier *Independence*. This was part of a Nato gathering in which British, Greek, Italian and Turkish warships were represented. We also discovered that the two yellow funneler was the state yacht *Savarona*. Our fare was under 20 pence - unless you paid a small surcharge for the express service. Three of the party were so caught but the rest of us went unnoticed.

Next, we boarded a coal burner to sail under the new bridge. She was probably French, as her engines came from Dunkirk. She took us to Beyirbeli where another vessel was approaching. This we boarded without a gangway - a commonplace occurrence here, though this skipper seemed a bit displeased. Our trip, passing under the new suspension bridge in both directions, provided us with excellent viewing. It was near 6.00 when we set off through the rush hour traffic for showers and a brief rest before going out to eat. We were surprised and impressed to note that they had cleaned the dust and debris under the beds! We tried several restaurants and eventually ate well. However, we left out the costly wine, as we had discovered a much cheaper local shop round the corner. The boss here had been a star footballer in his day though he was modest, even antagonistic, when we began to question him. We finished our day with an omelette at the hostel.

Donald and Bill took the bus to a garage to have the differential checked, according to plan. There a Turk drove them around the streets in a fearsome style and then pronounced the vehicle to be quite normal. Thereafter, Billco did his own servicing for the return trip home.

Our coalburner for the return trip

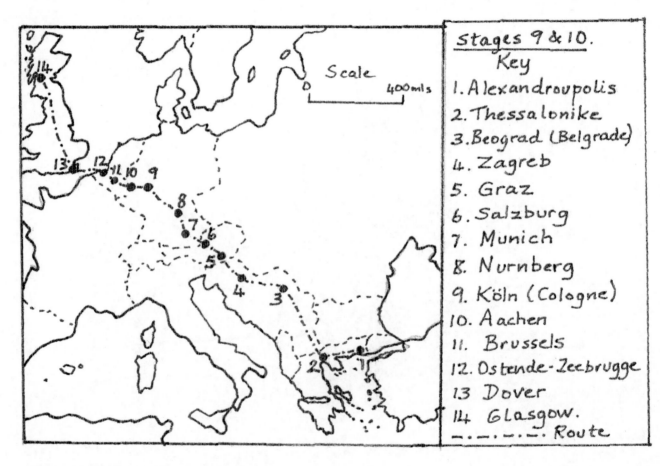

Scale
400 mls

Stages 9 & 10.
Key
1. Alexandroupolis
2. Thessalonike
3. Beograd (Belgrade)
4. Zagreb
5. Graz
6. Salzburg
7. Munich
8. Nurnberg
9. Köln (Cologne)
10. Aachen
11. Brussels
12. Ostende-Zeebrugge
13 Dover
14 Glasgow.
–..–..–..–.. Route

Stage 9

Friday 3 August - Monday 6 August

From Istanbul to Thessalonike; then Beograd and so into Austria and Bavaria

We were all roused by 5.30 and found it surprisingly dark. After showering, we packed using the toilet lighting and drove away within the hour. Roger was last to appear, somewhat dishevelled, from his separate dorm. Traffic was light and we were soon past the Londra campsite where Donald had previously thought to take us. Our hostel in the centre had proved much more convenient for our purpose. The sun was rising at Topkapi Gate as we departed Istanbul. We had a garage stop for breakfast at 8.00 and also purchased fresh bread to keep body and soul together during travel. Passing Ipsala, we were soon at the frontier zone for entry into Greece. Form filling was required of us at both frontiers but our passage was rapid. We narrowly escaped a bump at the frontier post when a German almost reversed into us, declaring that he failed to notice the bus!

Greek roads proved better than expected and we made good time to Alexandroupolis for 11.00. There we had business with the banks, as the frontier bank had been low in cash. The girl teller in the bank was sceptical about my passport photo and cheekily asked if I was father to the younger members of the group! The islands ferry *Samothrace* arrived at the same time as we made our appearance. Noon was approaching and we made this our lunch stop. We were tempted by word of a wine festival in the town but our timetable forbade. Instead, we sped on to arrive at Kavala for 3.30. The town is attractively located in a bay and with a Byzantine castle on its acropolis. The two storey Turkish aqueduct dating to the 16th century adds to its photo appeal. We had no time to spare but pushed on to Thessalonike. A rash of political signs and slogans appeared along the roadside. Kingship and the rule of the Colonels were the main topic, a live issue in 1973.

Cloud came over as the day advanced. Our route took us past the site of Amphipolis, an important Greek stronghold and later a staging post on Rome's Via Egnatia. A monumental stone lion marked the site, just next the river Strymon. We paused there for photographs. Then we were held up in a stramash between Greek road workers and a driver who had bumped a road worker without causing injury but arousing plenty annoyance. There was a noisy exchange of opinion, as other road users became involved. We stayed aloof and got on our way as soon as the dust had settled. As we waited to get going, Campbell realised that he was without his sleeping sheet. We surmised that it had been mistakenly removed from his bed in the Istanbul hostel along with their other laundry. Another bridge to cross in the days ahead!

Thessalonike was reached by 7.00 and the normal accommodation search got under way. We tried the tourist police and were told that the hostel was full but were presented with a list of hotels to try. We did the rounds and ended up at the Pantheon, paying rather more than we had hoped. Donald kept out of the haggling though he was our best Greek

Lion of Amphipolis at the River Strymon

speaker. The Pantheon turned out quite a good choice and was very clean. The kitty was running low, as petrol in Greece is dearer again, at over £5 per tankful. Six of us set out to find dinner. We varied our premises, starting with egg lemon soup in one place and going on to enjoy a huge slab of fish in another. Retsina, that Greek delight, was the drink of choice and we turned in at 11.00.

We were roused soon after 6.00 on Saturday by the cries of the hotel boss whom we had asked to give us a shout in the morning. He played his part diligently. Campbell rushed out before the reveille, as he was keen to see a bit of the city. He managed to reach the famous White Tower, sole survivor of the seaward defences, and the Arch of Galerius. Rain fell in the night but it was fine again by morning. We all contributed to the hotel bill to lighten the burden on the fast diminishing general kitty. After a hasty breakfast, we left the city by 7.00 and headed north towards the frontier with Jugoslavia. A new motorway with good lighting was under construction towards Evzone at the frontier and no doubt tolls will follow. We took breakfast at Evzone at a campsite restaurant. A small supply of retsina seemed a sound investment as we left Greece. The border crossing was speedy and we noticed that the pound's value was taking a hard knock when we changed money. The pound seemed to be sinking rather than floating! We came upon a top class Motel for lunch in Jugoslavia though service was painfully slow. Its prices were very fair, considering it was designed for tourists. Meaty soup and mushroom omelettes were popular. I had now reached the Epilogue in *War and Peace* and soon would be joining the card players. The weather was bad as we drove through Jugoslavia, with heavy showers accompanied by lightning.

Darkness had fallen by the time we reached Beograd and traffic was heavy. Worse still, the windscreen wipers failed us amid the rain and we fought our way to the campsite over a level crossing and up and down a selection of poorly lit back streets. Billco got to work on the wipers with success, while the rest of us unloaded our tents from the roof. We were far from happy about camping in the rain but fortunately the weather improved at the critical moment and we got the tents up in reasonably dry conditions. Timber chalets had seemed attractive till we heard the price and decided that we must all share the pain under canvas! David and Douglas, the snorers, were sleeping in the van and so less affected, though David mucked in with the rest and helped erect the tents. After cold showers, we got to the camp restaurant for 10.00. The menu was good though pricy. Only the gristly meat proved a disappointment.

This would seem to be a feature in Jugoslavia, as we had encountered the same problem with gristly goulash on our outward journey. Wine was expensive, so we settled for beer.

Next day saw the main party awake by 7.00. David and Douglas beat us to it, as they did not wish to be accused of holding up departure, especially when they had the privilege of sleeping in the bus! But George was up even earlier to shout and curse at reception for their noisy music, which began at 5 am. They only went so far as to shut the door to reduce the din. This camp differed from most others in that everyone seemed to be on the move very early and this explained the early activity at reception. We followed a circuitous route as we sought the city centre - we had found it hard the previous night finding the campsite.

The Glens lads had expressed a desire to visit the Military Museum and Donald dutifully found it for them. Various war engines from different eras were arrayed around the grounds - Roman, Byzantine, Turkish etc. The war enthusiasts got entry into the main building at 9.00 while Ian and I made our way to the river to see an old paddler now serving as a restaurant. She was named *Brod Split,* or at least that was the restaurant's name! She is moored on the river Sava before the junction with the Danube. Nothing would do but a meal aboard and we breakfasted in style after some difficulty with communication. The old ship seemed to hail from Dresden. Her decking was in poor, indeed precarious, condition and she was bereft of paddle wheels and engines. Fairy lights ran up to her funnel top. Two new Tourist cruise boats were moored alongside.

The bus picked us up at the bridge as we had arranged and we set off at once. The lads were very impressed by their visit to the museum and provided us with full details of what they had seen. We had to club together to finance the next tank of petrol and obviously the kitty needed to be replenished. The road condition was very variable over long distances and often was reduced to a single lane in each direction. This made overtaking a problem, especially when encountering farm vehicles. Cobbles were frequent and these sometimes roughly covered over, making them rather worse if anything! After Zagreb, we pressed on for the frontier amid showers, though the weather improved towards evening. We had a rowdy, argumentative game of cards, if game is the right description. This was followed by another dispute over our overnight stops on the next two nights. Ian was at his fiercest and Roger at his most determined. The decision, reached after prolonged and heated debate, was for one night each in Austria and Germany. Beer seemed to have some influence on the decision!

River Sava in Beograd from War Museum

It was fully 7.00 when we reached the frontier. The Jugo officer was very swift but his counterpart in Austria was a slower beast altogether. Once into Austria, we started to watch out for a suitable Gasthaus. None was forthcoming and by Graz we began to consider campsites. We left the main road while continuing towards Salzburg. This proved fortunate, as we came upon the Gasthaus Schweitzerhof at the roadside. Alasdair informed us that the name meant Black Yard. Whatever the omen, we were determined to stop. A plump Austrian lady came out, considered our position and enthusiastically directed us to a large mowed field across the road. Beside this was a river and, perhaps less attractive, a garage - not one, I might add, in any way likely to help with our differential concerns. We immediately accepted the proposal, parked the bus and unloaded the tents. There was to be no charge for this location. Up till now, the frau had only met three of us when we had explained what we required. So she was not a little surprised when our number had now jumped to eleven for dinner. We ate royally if expensively on soup and various meat dishes washed down with beer. The Gasthaus closed at midnight and this suited us well. As yesterday, we were back to three in the big tent. Throwing caution to the winds, we did not put up our flysheet.

We rose later than usual next morning, undisturbed by the nearby railway or passing traffic. Billco remarked that a van had driven up during the night and flashed his lights at us - perhaps the garage owner? We washed in the cool flow of the nearby river and availed ourselves of the toilets in the Gasthaus. Thus refreshed and after a ritual coffee, we took our leave around 9.00, enjoying the Austrian scenery in the morning sun. We all felt well rested, though soon the sun got higher and

Ready to strike camp at Gasthaus

humidity increased. By 12.00 we were in a traffic jam. A lorry driven by a Turk had gone off the road at a sharp bend and another lorry was attempting to heave it out the ditch, thus blocking the other lane. Two police officers watched the proceedings and held up the traffic. We cheekily got involved and managed to get our lane moving again and left the police to clear the other lane. They seemed quite unconcerned, perhaps even pleased by our contribution! We lost the best part of an hour in this guddle.

On reaching Salzburg, we parked and split up into groups. Ian and I had a snack at a riverside restaurant - the toilet there impressed us as it had a ray to signal automatic water flush after use - before taking a look at the city museum. I sent off a final postcard home and rejoined the bus after the allotted 3 hours. Hillbill had his eye on a cuckoo clock until he found the price. Even a DIY kit for a cuckoo clock was beyond his acceptable budget. Alasdair fared better and picked up a good German war book. On reaching the frontier, the Austrians made no attempt to delay us, while the Germans ignored our passports and were more eager to chat about our experiences. Sterling had made a slight improvement when we called at the frontier bank. So now we were in Bavaria and on the hunt again for an overnight stop.

We drove till 8.00 when we landed on a guesthouse at a crossroads, by Meisbach a little south of München (Munich). The interior was upmarket and the atmosphere stiff. However, the barrier dropped when we explained our need. Once again, we were told to park in the adjacent field and to use the toilets when we were ready to come for dinner. Again, there was no charge to park and again we ate well if expensively. We felt well filled when we rose from the table. The boss allowed us to carry out beer in steins to our tents and thus fuelled a lively evening in the field. Campbell was severely mocked when he contrived to pour half the contents of his beer glass over himself. The loss of his sleeping sheet in Istanbul added to his discomfiture and he was assured of a damp night in prospect. Still, our stops in Austria and Bavaria had now been successfully achieved, in line with our combatants' demands. The homeward run was beckoning.

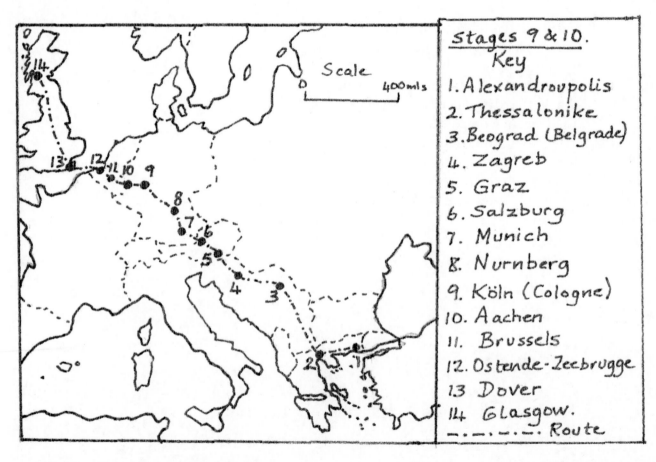

Scale

400 mls

Stages 9 & 10.

Key

1. Alexandroupolis
2. Thessalonike
3. Beograd (Belgrade)
4. Zagreb
5. Graz
6. Salzburg
7. Munich
8. Nurnberg
9. Köln (Cologne)
10. Aachen
11. Brussels
12. Ostende-Zeebrugge
13. Dover
14. Glasgow.
–..–..–..–. Route

Stage 10

Tuesday 7 August - Thursday 9 August

Out of Germany; across the Channel and back to Glasgow

Fine weather continued and we had a cooler evening under canvas. I slept soundly till 7.00. Before leaving, we returned our empty steins to the Gasthof. Its doors were still locked but after we had struck camp and loaded the tents (my shirt included as it transpired!), the doors were open and I had a wash. I found myself shirtless and everything firmly packed up aloft. Fortunately, Hillbill came to the rescue with a spare shirt in hand. Otherwise, we would have had to unload the roof and we certainly wanted to avoid this. We made a detour to avoid München and its traffic and then made for Nürnberg. Our breakfast stop was made on the motorway, followed by a fill for the bus. A tank of Super shell cost us the princely sum of nearly £8, a new record. Another symptom of that floating pound, perhaps? Lunch too was extortionate at a motorway stop. Rain returned with a vengeance in the afternoon and once again the wipers failed to respond. Fortunately, the rain was short lived. Traffic was heavy as we made our way past Köln, reaching Aachen at 8.30. Another campsite was located, this time an official one! We enjoyed much needed hot showers before setting out in quest of food. Our needs were met by a Decker Bier shop close to the camp and we ate well. Thereafter we enjoyed a few beers.

Up at 7.00 for showers and greeted by a dry, cool morning. News of a threatened strike by railway workers speeded up our departure towards the Channel and we were away within the hour. Soon we were in Belgium and changing money at the frontier. Everyone was involved this time, as the kitty was again in dire straits. The new Brussels to Ostend motorway was of a high standard, though service stations and rest places were in short supply. Eventually, we found a café at an Esso station and we had a quick breakfast stop. On reaching Ostend, we priced the liquor but found the prices unappealing and chose rather to look for gifts. Our ferry was from Zeebrugge and we were there half an hour before sailing time. Donald had earlier accepted a crossing time in the evening but Ian intervened and had us transferred to the afternoon crossing.

The tank was low but petrol prices high and so we took only a small amount to see us into Britain. *Free Enterprise V*, which also served us on the outward sailing, awaited us at the port and we boarded promptly. As the sun still shone, we sat out on deck for a time. I alone remained loyal to my shorts for the crossing. The fare back was £68, an increase of £8 on the outward fare. Everyone paid a final £5 into the kitty, making a final bill of £65 for each of us as our contribution.

At Dover we were directed somewhat ominously to the coach area, which was quite empty. There, we were instructed to walk through the customs, carrying all belongings including gifts and requiring us to unload the roof baggage. This, it transpired, was the acid test. Donald was then waved through without further ado when and only when we and our kit attracted no interest. Even George's Afghan coat passed without comment. We

Newport Pagnall Services: The gang returns to reality

had tea at Dover, some going for Chinese, even as they had done on the first day of the trip, all those days back. There was a campsite outside the town and we made this our goal. The site was well priced and quiet. Most of us made phone calls home before bedding down for the last night.

So this was to be our homecoming, Thursday 9 August, after 6 weeks of travel and hardly a harsh word! The morning was fine and we gave the bus a good clean out so that we could get all away sharp on reaching Glasgow. We set out on the road north soon after 6.30, with a breakfast stop to follow. We were through the Dartford tunnel by 9.00. The second tunnel was under construction and certainly needed to cope with the heavy traffic. The existing lanes were crammed nose to tail. Our next brief stop on the motorway was Newport Pagnall and it all seemed something of an anticlimax after the places and menus we had experienced hitherto. Then we turned in at Manchester to deposit Ian outside his house there. It was just after 3.00. There were already plenty new M registered cars on the motorway as we headed north. Squally showers began after Manchester and there was evidence of flooding in the fields and along riverbanks.

We made one more, short stop for sustenance before our arrival at Glasgow St Enoch, which was thought best suited to our different destinations. Our arrival in the city was 8.40 pm. We unloaded the roof and thanked the weatherman for favouring us with dry if windy conditions. Then we said our farewells and made our separate arrangements for getting away. At the start of the trip, the mileometer read 8897 and had now advanced to 20,481. So the whole voyage of discovery had covered 11,584 miles. All that remained was to hand out our assorted gifts and return the bus to the High School. It was a bit travel worn but Donald, assisted by Billco, had driven it impeccably and got us back without so much as a scrape.

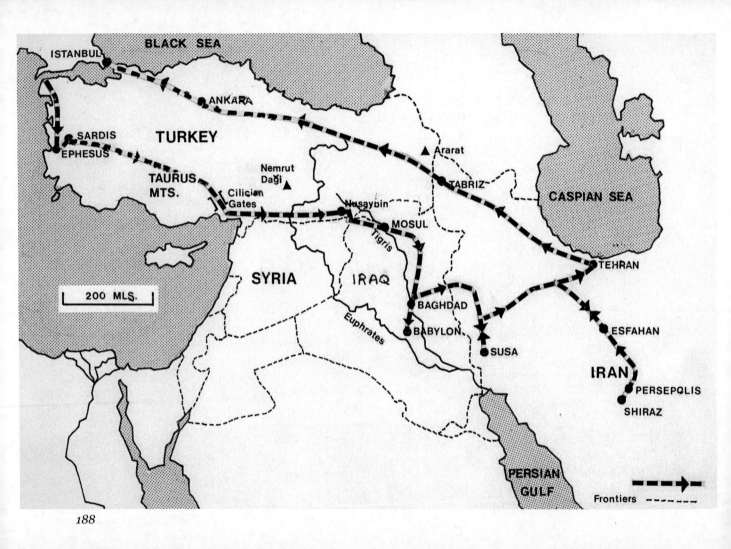

In Retrospect

The **vehicle** first deserves special praise, having covered all of the 11,500 miles with only minor upsets, and carrying the name of the High School of Glasgow through Europe and the Middle East. Even when the quality of petrol was poor, the bus soldiered on, overheating on the hills, it is true, but always pressing ahead. The differential was our chief worry as early as Nemrut Dağı and worsening a little as we progressed into Iran. Yet it never failed us, even when we could find no major garage on the trip to give it the thorough check which we believed was required. It was only at Nemrut that we lost confidence and decided to leave the bus and make alternative transport arrangements. When this attempt to find a garage to deal with the suspected problem failed, we never really lost faith again - though we did worry!

Billco deserved our praise for his able intervention in matters of greasing, engine cleaning, oil changes and general maintenance. The stone through the windscreen in Bulgaria was unfortunate and unavoidable but Turkey saw us right with a new, effective replacement. It was as well that we had carried a temporary screen to tide us over till we could fit that replacement! The road surfaces frequently were bad and caused a judder with the steering wheel, but this could be tholed. Then there were the lapses by the wipers in the occasional rain which we encountered. Here again, Billco proved his worth. We found rainwater coming in at the doors, probably thanks to settling over the long drive with a hefty load. This was to remain a problem for the bus when it was returned to the High School for more normal use. Numerous pupils were to comment on this water feature in the years ahead. We had left our mark! Interestingly, there was never a murmur about the differential, although that had been our greatest worry on the trip.

Now to the **members of the group**. Donald could not be faulted for his planning of the route nor for his driving competence. To have brought the bus back without a scratch, despite rough roads, mountain passes, frenetic driving conditions and appalling drivers says it all! His calm acceptance of situations was invaluable when there were problems, if exasperating when decisions were required. Even the threat of immediate imprisonment in Iran in the event of a road accident left him apparently unaffected. Seeking help in finding the way to places was not his style

at all and he preferred to keep going, in the hope of a good outcome or leaving others to make enquiries when these became crucial. Changes of route or requests to visit special locations were accepted without demur. He was more into camping than any of us and was frequently overruled by the group when more comfortable accommodation was available at an affordable rate. He was less likely to eat out, preferring often to cook at a campsite when others went for restaurants. His tendency to stay in the bus, when the main party was engaged in site visits, was a little surprising. Perhaps he had built up such a strong rapport with the vehicle that he found it hard to tear himself away! But the real explanation should be put down to his dislike of heat and we certainly encountered a lot of this.

Billco tended to follow Donald's lead in most matters, but came into his own in the area of bus maintenance. We had him to thank for the smooth running of the vehicle and it would certainly not have been his fault had the differential actually failed. Like Bruce and the spider, he kept trying and trying to get expert advice. His insect repellents and insecticide sprays were often invaluable. Insect bites gave him a bad reaction, hence he had some useful expertise in this area. Douglas and David as a rule joined Donald and Bill when at campsites, whereas Alasdair was more of a wild card and spread his favours around the group! George tended to be a bit clumsy and occasionally thoughtless and his snoring proved annoying, except to Alasdair who sometimes shared the same failing. The two of them shared a tent when in campsites, while David and Douglas, the really effective snorers, made the bus their usual refuge. Ian, sometimes known for a short temper in previous trips, was exemplary on this one and a very valuable confidant so far as I was concerned. Hillbill was constantly cheery and totally dependable when it came to getting things done, such as marshalling tents etc. He accepted plenty ribbing for his assortment of pills and potions. He actually abandoned his anti sunburn tablets when he found they were so effective as to leave him totally unaffected by the sun! Even when suffering nose bleeds and sickness, he refused to concede. Roger proved a great sport and entered into the spirit of everything enthusiastically, while Campbell started quiet and became gradually more outspoken and dogmatic.

The whole group blended well and disagreements were rare. This was quite remarkable, considering the distance travelled in hot conditions and in confined quarters for so much of the time.

Our **reception** in the various countries was interesting. As I have said, we tended to wear shorts for travelling and longs for walking in cities. Long trousers were a requirement when we were visiting religious centres. The sight of a group of bare chested males spilling out of a minibus was unusual anywhere, but caused quite a stir in Turkey, Iraq and Iran where foreigners were less commonly seen, especially partially clad ones! Occasionally, while visiting open sites, we were asked by custodians to cover up. This we did with some reluctance. But it was in small towns and villages that we caused a minor sensation and attracted onlookers of all ages. People were almost always very friendly, and not just to attract custom in their hotels and restaurants. Perhaps Iraqis above all impressed me with their friendliness, eagerness to assist and their command of English. Iran came off badly by comparison, where people were often aloof and showed little willingness to communicate.

We were definitely lucky in **health matters**. Of course, every one of us suffered upset stomach at some point and toilet calls and atrocious hygiene could be a problem. Often we were caught short at frontier posts and there we were always sympathetically treated. We shared their facilities although these were often far from impressive. No one suffered severe sunburn, though both on the climb up Nemrut Dağı and at Persepolis itself we took a pasting. Hillbill swore by Silvasun for his protection and at first he treated himself to quite a galaxy of tablets. He reduced intake as the trip progressed. Donald and Roger alone did not use antimalarial tablets and seemed none the worse for the omission. We ignored the sensible medical advice about eating carefully and enjoyed regular salads and cold food such as ice cream and chilled drinks. Why, we even cut raw ice to add to our water bottles!

We managed to keep ourselves reasonably clean during the trip despite the heat and frequent dust. Showers were often hard to achieve but we usually managed to get access to water. Strict budgeting too was a factor when it came to showering: additional charges were usually rejected and use of hand basins was preferred! Gaziantep was one of the most difficult places for getting water, and washing clothes was everywhere problematical. A couple of campsites spoiled us by providing swimming pools and we were rarely near enough the sea to enjoy a bathe.

And so to **costs**. I suggested at the outset that spending money should be set at £105 minimum for the expected six weeks. This would include a small element for gifts and sundries with drinks, soft and otherwise, making the greatest demands. The main contribution from the total was £65 towards the kitty, leaving £35 for gifts etc. Today, it seems a tiny amount and yet, looking back to my trips to Greece for students in 1962, it appears quite realistic. Further, everyone could expect a small rebate at the conclusion: Donald was left with a fair quantity of unspent foreign currency left in the kitty; we still had a small insurance rebate to repay, and there was money expected from the AA for our hire of an enlarged tool kit which was returned almost entire. Billco reckoned he spent about £105 on vehicle maintenance. We made no claim at all on the Glasgow Corporation personal insurance nor, of course, did we have reason to call on the indemnity bond, as we brought the bus back, safe and reasonably sound, from Iran.

Petrol was naturally the main drain on the kitty. A tankful in Germany came in highest at around £7.50 and even £8. Runner up was Austria at £5.50 and Greece closely behind at £5. Jugoslavia stood at around £4, though here alone petrol coupons were available to encourage tourism and effected a small reduction. Turkey charged around £3, though often the petrol was lower octane and the bus hated this and performed accordingly. Iraq and Iran were lowest, each charging around £2 for a full tank. For comparison, in Britain we paid £4.50 to fill the tank. The range of different currencies in these days before the euro added to the interest of paying at garages, hotels and restaurants as we moved from one country to another.

Conclusion

This was to be my last overland schools excursion of this type, as marriage would change my holiday pattern. Then again, Strathclyde Region came into being in 1975 and with it a stricter regimen. I doubt whether such a venture would have been supported or allowed, considering the obstacles and risks. But I reckon that all of us who participated gained greatly from the experience and had no regrets. As for myself, I was able to use my slides to support the new course for Classical studies which I was piloting on the topic "The Greeks and the Persians." That, you may recall, had been a major factor in the original plan.

Francis Bacon observed "Travel, in the younger sort, is a part of education; in the elder, a part of experience." Our overland excursion to Persepolis certainly bore this out.

Acknowledgements

In the preparation and execution of our itinerary in 1973, two books in Hachette's World Guides were crucial, providing a fund of valuable information and guidance. These were:

Turkey, originally written by Robert Boulanger, 1970 edition and *The Middle East*, originally by Robert Boulanger, 1966 edition.

For more historical detail and intrinsic interest, I referred also to:

A History of the Persian Empire, Olmstead, University of Chicago Press, 1970 edition - a quite remarkable work.

Also *Persia: An Archaeological Guide* by Sylvia Matheson (Faber, 1971).

The Hachette Guides remained invaluable for refreshing my memory when preparing this publication of my diary. I was further assisted by my friend Roger McIlroy, who had himself accompanied the 1973 trip as a student and kept his own account. I have referred a couple of times in my text to his comments and am also indebted to him for two photographs of me on the trip.

Finally there was need of maps to identify our routes and here my long standing friend and former geography teacher Highet Rodger came to the rescue and produced maps for various stages in our travel.

For the rest, the text and photographs are my own and I have to thank family and friends for encouraging me to publish.

Index

Fellow travellers are indexed under their first names.